1 Maccabees

Guides to Apocrypha and Pseudepigrapha
Series Editor
Michael A. Knibb

1 MACCABEES

John R. Bartlett

Sheffield
Academic Press

Copyright © 1998 Sheffield Academic Press

Published by Sheffield Academic Press Ltd
Mansion House
19 Kingfield Road
Sheffield S11 9AS
England

Printed on acid-free paper in Great Britain
by The Cromwell Press
Trowbridge, Wiltshire

British Library Cataloguing in Publication Data

A catalogue record for this book is available
from the British Library

ISBN 1-85075-763-1

Contents

Preface

This study guide attempts to introduce the reader to an ancient text known, if at all, through the collection of writings called the Apocrypha. This guide begins by asking where this document came from and how it reached us, and takes the reader back from the printed Apocrypha of the Christian Bible via the earlier Latin and Greek manuscripts to the origins of 1 Maccabees in a late second or early first century BCE Jewish text, probably written in Hebrew. Chapter 2 studies the text as it is and explores its structure and composition, and its author's aims and theology. As the author has historical interests, and like many other historians in the Bible and elsewhere, is much concerned with dates, Chapter 3 examines the complexities of the dating system or systems used in the book, and studies the chronology and sequence of events as presented by 1 Maccabees. After these important preliminaries, the following chapters turn to the story itself, examining topics of major interest to students of the Maccabaean period—among others, the decree of Antiochus IV, the 'abomination of desolation', the campaigns of Judas, the death of Antiochus, the cleansing of the sanctuary and the Maccabaean diplomatic relationships with Rome.

This study guide is not a commentary on 1 Maccabees, and does not attempt to give detailed notes on the many events and people crowding its pages. For such information the reader is referred to the proper sources. Although the study of Maccabaean history must involve close analysis of 2 Maccabees as well (not to mention Daniel and Josephus), this guide restricts itself largely to 1 Maccabees (though noting its differences from 2 Maccabees). Its aim is not to provide a comprehensive synthesis of the Maccabaean period, but to understand the picture of events given by the author of 1 Maccabees; 2 Maccabees is a very different work, and will be studied separately in another volume of this series.

1 Maccabees provides an entrée to a much larger world than that of second-century BCE Judah. It is full of reference to the wider world around it, from Persia in the east to Rome in the west. In recent years,

there has been an upsurge of interest in the Hellenistic world and its influence upon the Jews, both at home and abroad. The Jews became part of that Hellenistic world, and the Maccabaean revolution was part of a wider history. For those who want to see the Maccabaean movement in context, Peter Green's *Alexander to Actium: The Hellenistic Age* will be found an invaluable and lasting companion, a treasure house in its own right.

John R. Bartlett
Dublin, July 1997

Text, Translations and Commentaries, and Other Major Works

Editions of the Greek and Latin Texts

R. Gryson and R. Weber (ed.), *Biblia Sacra iuxta vulgatam versionem* (Stuttgart: Deutsche Bibelgesellschaft, 4th edn, 1984)

W. Kappler (ed.), *Maccabaeorum liber I, Septuaginta, Vetus Testamentum Graecum Auctoritate Societatis Litterarum Gottingensis, vol. IX, fasc.1* (Göttingen: Vandenhoeck & Ruprecht, 2nd rev. edn, 1967)

A. Rahlfs, *Septuaginta id est V.T. graece iuxta LXX interpretes. I. Leges et Historiae* (Stuttgart, 1935)

H.B. Swete, *The Old Testament in Greek according to the Septuagint*, III (Cambridge: Cambridge University Press, 1894).

Translations and Commentaries

F.-M. Abel, *Les livres des Maccabées* (Paris: Gabalda, 1949). A classic and detailed commentary of first-class scholarship, complete with Greek text.

F.-M. Abel and J. Starcky, *Les livres des Maccabées* (La Sainte Bible; Paris: Cerf, 3rd edn, 1961). A useful brief and clear commentary.

J.R. Bartlett, *The First and Second Books of the Maccabees* (Cambridge Bible Commentary;.Cambridge: Cambridge University Press, 1973). An introductory but detailed commentary for students.

J.C. Dancy, *A Commentary on 1 Maccabees* (Oxford: Basil Blackwell, 1954). This commentary by a classical scholar has good critical discussion of the text.

J. Goldstein, *I Maccabees* (Anchor Bible, 41; Garden City, NY: Doubleday, 1976). A major, detailed commentary by a scholar with wide-ranging grasp of the literature.

C.L.W. Grimm, *Das erste Buch der Maccabäer* (Kurzgefasstes exegetische; Handbuch zu den Apokryphen des Alten Testaments; ed. O.F. Fritsche; Leipzig: Hirzel, 1853). An early and still valuable critical study.

W.O.E. Oesterley, '1 Maccabees' in R.H. Charles (ed.), *The Apocrypha and Pseudepigrapha of the Old Testament in English. I. Apocrypha* (Oxford: Clarendon Press, 1913). A precise, classical commentary based on the Revised Version.

S. Tedesche and S. Zeitlin, *The First Book of Maccabees* (New York: Harper, for Dropsie College, 1950). This is a useful book, containing the Greek text, with English translation, an introduction and appendices, and limited notes.

Other Important Works

B. Bar-Kochva, *Judas Maccabaeus: The Jewish Struggle against the Seleucids* (Cambridge: Cambridge University Press, 1989). In spite of the title, this valuable book is concerned primarily with military matters.

E. Bickermann, *Der Gott der Makkabäer* (Berlin: Schocken Verlag/Jüdischer Buchverlag, 1937); English translation: H.R. Moehring *The God of the Maccabees*, (Leiden: E.J. Brill, 1979). Bickermann set the agenda for several decades by highlighting the contribution of the extreme Jewish Hellenists to the origins of the Maccabaean struggle.

K. Bringmann, *Hellenistische Reform und Religionsverfolgung in Judäa* (AAWG; Philologische-historische Klasse, 3rd series 132; Göttingen: Vandenhoeck & Ruprecht, 1983). This study is important both for matters of dating and for the interpretation of the Maccabaean rebellion. It lays much blame for events on the high-priest Menelaus.

W.D. Davies and L. Finkelstein (eds.), *The Cambridge History of Judaism*. II. *The Hellenistic Age* (Cambridge: Cambridge University Press, 1989). This includes useful essays on Antiochus IV (O. Mørkholm) and on the Hasmonaean revolt (J.A. Goldstein).

L. Grabbe, *Judaism from Cyrus to Hadrian* (London: SCM Press, 1992). This comprehensive student textbook provides an excellent introduction to every aspect of the Maccabaean age.

Peter Green, *Alexander to Actium: The Hellenistic Age* (London: Thames & Hudson, 1990). This encyclopaedic and exciting synthesis of the Hellenistic Age offers a superb introduction to the wider context of the Maccabaean rebellion, and includes an excellent chapter on Hellenism and the Jews.

M. Hengel, *Judaism and Hellenism* (London, SCM Press, 1974). A detailed scholarly examination of the impact of Hellenism on the Jews.

O. Mørkholm, *Antiochus IV of Syria* (Classica et Medievalia, Dissertationes, 8; Copenhagen: Gyldendalske Boghandel, 1966). The standard modern work on Antiochus IV.

P. Schäfer, 'The Hellenistic and Maccabaean Periods', in J.H. Hayes and J.M. Miller, *Israelite and Judaean History* (London: SCM Press, 1977), pp. 539-604.

E. Schürer, *A History of the Jewish People in the Time of Jesus Christ* (Edinburgh: T. & T. Clark, 1885–91); revised English edn: G. Vermes, F. Millar and M. Black, *The History of the Jewish People in the Age of Jesus Christ (175 BC–AD 135)* (3 vols.; Edinburgh: T. & T. Clark, 1973–87). A standard work of reference.

V. Tcherikover, *Hellenistic Civilization and the Jews* (trans. S. Applebaum; Philadelphia: The Jewish Publication Society of America; Jerusalem: The Magnes Press, The Hebrew University, 1959). Tcherikover's stimulating book argues that hellenization in Judaea was resisted by the Hasidim, and that Antiochus's persecution was provoked by Jewish revolt (rather than vice versa).

Abbreviations

AAWG	Abhandlungen der Akademie der Wissenschaften zu Göttingen
ABD	Anchor Bible Dictionary
AJP	*American Journal of Philology*
AV	Authorized Version
BA	*Biblical Archaeologist*
BAIAS	*Bulletin of the Anglo-Israel Archaeological Society*
BASOR	*Bulletin of the American Schools of Oriental Research*
BZAW	Beihefte zur ZAW
CP	*Classical Philology*
HSCP	*Harvard Studies in Classical Philology*
HUCA	*Hebrew Union College Annual*
IEJ	*Israel Exploration Journal*
JBL	*Journal of Biblical Literature*
JJS	*Journal of Jewish Studies*
JSHRZ	Jüdische Schriften aus hellenistisch-römische Zeit
JSJ	*Journal for the Study of Judaism in the Persian, Hellenistic and Roman Period*
JSOTSup	*Journal for the Study of the Old Testament*, Supplement Series
JSP	*Journal for the Study of the Pseudepigrapha*
JSS	*Journal of Semitic Studies*
JTS	*Journal of Theological Studies*
MH	*Museum Helveticum*
NEB	New English Bible
NRSV	New Revised Standard Version
PEQ	*Palestine Exploration Quarterly*
RB	*Revue biblique*
REB	Revised English Bible
RSV	Revised Standard Version
RV	Revised Version
SBL	Society of Biblical Literature
TTZ	*Trierer Theologische Zeitschrift*
VT	*Vetus Testamentum*
ZAW	*Zeitschrift für die alttestamentliche Wissenschaft*

1

THE ORIGIN OF 1 MACCABEES

The Apocrypha

The first questions that should be asked of any important document, ancient or modern, are those of origin. Where did this document come from, and how did it get to us? Today we are familiar with 1 Maccabees as a book to be found among the writings of the Apocrypha. The Apocrypha contains Jewish writings dating from the period between the third century BCE and the first century CE and preserved in the Greek language. These writings, apart from the book known to us as 2 Esdras, were included by the early Greek-speaking Church in its Bible, the Septuagint, but they were not part of the Jewish canon of scripture, and this fact put an early question mark in some parts of the Church against their biblical status. Both Origen and Augustine understood 1 Maccabees to be outside the Jewish canon. In the fourth century CE the biblical scholar Jerome (c. 325–420 CE) translated most of the Christian scriptures from their original languages into Latin, but among the Jewish writings he distinguished between those found in the Hebrew canon and those found only in Greek, and the latter he described by the Greek word *apocrypha*, 'hidden (things)', or by the Latin phrase *libri ecclesiastici*, 'books of the church', which were not the same as *libri canonici*, 'canonical books'. In spite of Jerome, however, these books continued to be part of the Western Church's Latin Bible, the Vulgate, which included Jerome's translation of the Hebrew books along with the earlier, Old Latin, translation of the Greek books, and the inclusion of these books was confirmed at the Council of Trent (1545–63). The Vulgate (*editio vulgata*) provided the generally accepted text of the Christian Bible from the sixth century CE to the Reformation in the sixteenth century. It was handed down for centuries by a succession of manuscript copies; the first printed edition, which used Johann

Gutenberg's invention of movable type, was the 'Gutenberg' Bible of 1456.

The importance of the invention of printing for the Reformation is well known, and Martin Luther and others made good use of it for their tracts and controversial writings. The reformers were not particularly sympathetic towards *libri ecclesiastici*, and followed Jerome in distinguishing them from books of the Hebrew canon. In Luther's Bible (1534) the apocryphal books (apart from 1 and 2 Esdras) were seen as 'useful and good to be read' (but not inspired) and were printed as an appendix; Coverdale's English Bible a year later similarly grouped the 'Apocrifa' together at the end of the Old Testament. In England the Calvinist-inspired Geneva (or 'Breeches') Bible (1560) included the apocryphal books, accepting them 'for their knowledge of history and instruction of godly manners', a phrase taken up in the Church of England's Thirty-Nine Articles of Religion, which state (Article VI) that 'the other [i.e. apocryphal] books (as Hierome saith) the Church doth read for example of life and instruction of manners; but yet doth it not apply them to establish any doctrine'. In 1643, the Westminster Confession declared that the apocryphal books 'are of no authority in the Church of God, nor to be any otherwise approved or made use of than other human writings'. To this day the apocryphal books are preserved in a separate section, placed between Old and New Testaments, in Bible translations following the Protestant tradition (AV, RV, RSV and NRSV, NEB and REB). In recent years there has been considerable growth of scholarly interest in these writings, which have so much to tell us of Judaism between the third century BCE and the first century CE.

Behind the Printed Texts: The Manuscripts

For scholarly purposes, it is important to look back beyond the printed text found in our Bibles to discover where the printers found the text they copied. The text of the Vulgate, first printed at Mainz in the Gutenberg Bible, is represented by a number of manuscripts from the eighth and ninth centuries; but the Latin text of 1 Maccabees depends basically on the Old Latin tradition, represented in particular by the manuscripts La^L (Lugdunensis, from Lyon, early ninth century) and La^X (Complutensis, Madrid, late ninth century). The Old Latin tradition ultimately goes back to the second or early third century CE, and so is of importance for the critical reconstruction of the early Greek text that it translated. Its particular importance lies in the fact that the Old Latin translation witnesses to the text of the Greek Bible before it was heavily revised by Lucian of Antioch, a biblical scholar and theologian martyred at Nicomedia in 312 CE.

The Greek text of 1 Maccabees was first printed in Cardinal Ximenes' Complutensian Polyglot in 1514–17 (Complutum was the Latin name of Alcalá in Spain). Ximenes wrote that he had taken the greatest care to base his text on the purest and most ancient manuscripts available (in fact, among others he used a fifteenth-century Venetian manuscript now preserved in Madrid, and two fourteenth-century manuscripts sent to him from the Vatican Library; details are given in H.B. Swete, *Introduction to the Old Testament in Greek*, 1902, p. 172; cf. pp. 155 [no. 68], 156 [no. 108], 157 [no. 248]). Ximenes could not use either the fourth-century Codex Vaticanus (B), which seems to have been in the Vatican Library by 1481, but did not include either 1 or 2 Maccabees, or Codex Sinaiticus, the fourth-century manuscript of the Greek Bible, which was unknown in the west until it was rediscovered at St Catherine's on Mt Sinai by Tischendorf in 1844. He did not know the fifth-century Codex Alexandrinus (A), which was presented to Charles I in London in 1627 from the Patriarch of Alexandria, or the important eighth-century Codex Venetus (V), which contains the Greek text of all four books known as 'Maccabees'. (Codex V is the second volume of Codex Basiliano-Vaticanus, whose first volume, N, is preserved at Rome; the second volume, V, was preserved in the Library of St Mark's at Venice. On this manuscript, see H.B. Swete, *The Old Testament in Greek*, III [1894], pp. xiv-xvi.) The three great 'uncial' manuscripts, Vaticanus, Sinaiticus and Alexandrinus, probably stem from the same archetypal text of the second or third century. 'Uncial' manuscripts were written in what might be described as large, capital letters; the less awkward cursive 'miniscule' script was developed in the ninth century. A number of miniscule manuscripts witness to the text of 1 Maccabees; one group of ten manuscripts, collectively known as q, may derive from a fourth-century text free of Lucianic influence; a second group represents the Lucianic text, and a third group has incorporated Lucianic readings. These latter two groups are thus less valuable as evidence for the earliest Greek text.

1 Maccabees also existed in Syriac and Armenian versions. Two Syriac manuscripts exist, one clearly based on a Lucianic Greek text and the other a correction of it. An edition of the Syriac text appears in the Polyglot Bible edited by Brian Walton (1600–61) and published in

London in 1653–57. The Armenian text appears to relate to the Old
Latin tradition rather than the Greek.

The Evidence of Josephus

In sum, the manuscript evidence for the text appears to take us back to
an early Latin translation used by the second-or third-century CE
Church (though some have suspected a Jewish translator), and to an
early Greek text, in both pre-Lucianic (i.e. the *q* group of miniscules
mentioned above) and Lucianic versions. The few references to and
quotations of 1 Maccabees in early Christian authors—Clement of
Alexandria, Hippolytus, Tertullian, Origen, Cyprian, Eusebius of
Caesarea—show that the two Maccabaean books, and their relationship
with events described in the book of Daniel, were known, but there is
little help here for the textual critic. Potentially more useful is the use
made of 1 Maccabees as a primary source by Josephus in *Antiquities*
12.242–13.212. In the *Jewish War*, where Josephus gives a short
description of the Maccabaean period as part of the background to the
Jewish war with Rome, Josephus used as the source for the
Maccabaean period the world history of Nicolaus of Damascus, a
Hellenistic historiographer who worked as ambassador and counsellor
at the court of Herod the Great. In *Antiquities*, however, Josephus sees
the Maccabaean period as part of the continuing history of the Jews,
and uses 1 Maccabees as his source, just as he had used the books of
Ezra and Esther as sources for the Persian period. 1 Maccabees was perhaps sufficiently like Scripture for Josephus's purpose, in that its author
presented events in a style reminiscent of the books of Judges and
Samuel. In *Contra Apionem* 1.7-8 (37-44) Josephus describes 22 Jewish
books accepted as historically trustworthy, and adds that 'from
Artaxerxes to our own day, the detailed history has been written, but it
has not been granted the same credibility as earlier writings, because
the prophetic succesion is not certainly established'. Josephus presumably has in mind here 1 Maccabees, as well as Hecataeus of Abdera, the
Letter of Aristeas and the works of Nicolaus of Damascus, and this suggests that, though Josephus was anxious to use 1 Maccabees as a Jewish
history for his own history of the Jews, he did not in fact see
1 Maccabees as Scripture.

Josephus does not simply copy 1 Maccabees, which he knew in a
Greek text, but paraphrases and expands his source, incorporating
material from other authors such as Polybius (the Greek historian, c.

203–120 BCE), Posidonios (c. 135–50 BCE), Diodorus (flourished c. 60–30 BCE), Nicolaus of Damascus and others. He rewrites speeches from 1 Maccabees, or invents new speeches for his characters; he removes Hebraic archaisms and explains Jewish dating by adding Greek equivalents. All this means that Jospehus is not particularly useful for establishing the original Greek text of 1 Maccabees; he would be much more useful to the textual critic if, as some suggest on the basis of certain passages, he knew also a Hebrew version of the book (see Tedesche and Zeitlin, The *First Book of Maccabees,* pp. 57-58). In either case, Josephus seems to have followed 1 Maccabees only as far as the end of ch. 13, returning at this point to follow the shorter version in the *Jewish War.* The reason for this has been much discussed. Some scholars have suggested that Josephus's copy of 1 Maccabees lacked its final scroll, and others that at this point Josephus preferred to use his other sources (mainly Nicolaus of Damascus), to which he would have to return for the reign of Hyrcanus. Abel notes (*Les livres des Maccabées,* 1949, p. xiv) that there are indications in *Antiquities* that Josephus did in fact know the material of 1 Maccabees 13–15 (compare *Ant.* 13.214 with 1 Macc. 14.4-15; *Ant.* 13.227 with 1 Macc. 14.24; 15.15; *Ant.* 13.223-25 with 1 Macc. 15.1-9, 25-31), and that Josephus had thus drawn as much from 1 Maccabees as he needed.

The evidence of Josephus, then, demonstrates clearly that 1 Maccabees, at least as far as ch. 13 and probably to ch. 16, was known and available to Josephus in its Greek form by the end of the first century CE. Josephus wrote his *Antiquities* in Rome, completing it in the thirteenth year of Domitian's reign (93–94 CE) (*Ant.* 20.12.1 [267]). It is perhaps most likely that Josephus acquired his copy of 1 Maccabees from Jerusalem before its destruction in 70 CE and took it with him to Rome; we cannot tell. He may have acquired it by the good offices of Jewish friends in Rome (perhaps his patron King Agrippa II, who wrote to him about his Jewish War, cf. *Life* 65; *Apion* 1.9), or perhaps even from a library in Rome.

The Original Hebrew Version

The Greek form of 1 Maccabees known to Josephus, however, was not the earliest form of the book, but a fairly literal translation into Septuagintal Greek from the original Hebrew. In the late second century CE Origen (cited in Eusebius, *Hist. Eccles.* 6.25) said that the book was entitled *Sarbēthsabanaiel*, which is perhaps the Greek transliteration

of the Aramaic version of an originally Hebrew title. Various recon-
structions of the original Hebrew have been offered. The most popular
is probably *spr byt hsmōn'ym*, 'The Book of the House of the
Hasmonaeans', to which it has been objected that the book itself does
not use the name 'Hasmonaean', which comes from Josephus, *War* 1.3;
Ant. 12.265); however, if, as has been suggested, the Hebrew original
of 'Hasmonaeus' was not a proper name but a word meaning 'prince',
the objection may be overruled. Another proposed reconstruction
offers *spr byt srḥy'l*, 'The Book of the House of the Princes of God', or,
if with one manuscript we read *iēl* as the final letters, treating them as
an abbreviation for *Israel*, *spr byt srḥy ysr'l*, 'The Book of the House of
the Princes of Israel'. J. Goldstein suggests an original *spr byt srbny'l*,
'The Book of the Dynasty of God's Resisters' (the Hebrew root *srb*
appears in participial form Ezek. 2.6 meaning 'briers'). The Hebrew
words underlying Origen's *sabanaiel* remain elusive, all proposals imply-
ing some degree of corruption or misunderstanding of the original
Hebrew, but the suggestion in these words of a Hebrew title is supported by Jerome's comment 'Macchabaeorum primum librum
hebraicum repperi' (*Prologus Galeatus*), which may perhaps be translated, 'I found the first book of Maccabees in Hebrew' (did Jerome
therefore know an extant Hebrew text of 1 Maccabees?), or possibly, 'I
found the first book of Maccabees to be a Hebrew book', which need
not suggest that Jerome had sight of a Hebrew text.

The existence of an Hebrew original of 1 Maccabees is further supported by the number and variety of Semitic idioms visible behind the
Greek translation; C.C. Torrey (Enc. Bib. III [1902], pp. 2858–59)
gives a large list of these, pointing especially to passages such as 1.29,
3.15-26, 5.1-8, 28-34, to transliterated names such as those in 11.34
and 39, to words transliterated but not understood by the translator in
14.29 and 12.37, and to errors that are the result of mistranslation or
accidental corruption of the underlying Hebrew, for example 8.29,
where the translator has translated a Hebrew perfect by a Greek aorist;
10.1, where the epithet *Epiphanes* is wrongly applied to Alexander the
son of Antiochus instead of to Antiochus, and 14.9, where the Greek
phrase *stolas polemou*, 'robes of war' (*ṣaba*), is inappropriate to a period
of paradisal peace, and perhaps should be translated 'ornamental robes'
(*ṣebi*). The Hebrew style of the writer is seen throughout the book,
and especially in the poetic passages such as 3.3-9. R.H. Pfeiffer suggested that the author was influenced by the work of the Chronicler,
and that he planned the book as a sequel to 1 and 2 Chronicles, Ezra

and Nehemiah, in order to bring the history of his people down to his own time. This would explain his archaic terminology, his incorporation of pious addresses and poems, and his use of official documents (cf. the book of Ezra).

It seems likely, then, that behind the Greek text known to Josephus lay a Hebrew original, presumably the text of the original author. That the author should have written about the creation of a new independent Israel in the national language of the Jews itself says something about his pride in his country and its leaders (he uses the ancient name 'Israel' over 40 times). That the book should have been translated into Greek early in its career—probably in the first century BCE—is evidence of the growing importance of Greek in the Jewish world. The Hasmonaean leaders themselves were not slow to incorporate some of the trappings of Hellenistic monarchies into their system, and King Alexander Jannaeus (103–76 BCE) not only used the name of Alexander the Great but produced bilingual coinage bearing the inscriptions 'Yehonathan the king' (Hebrew) and 'King Alexander' (Greek). A Greek translation of a book emphasizing the importance of the Hasmonaean monarchy in the latter-day history of Israel might have been welcome enough at the Hasmonaean court, and it might also have been welcome in some quarters of the Jewish diaspora abroad in places such as Alexandria, where the Hebrew scriptures had been translated into Greek. The Greek version of 1 Maccabees is written not in the colloquial style of the Greek Hellenistic world, in the language of the *Koinē*, but in the style of the Greek scriptures, the Septuagint, and the book may have been translated in this style as a deliberate attempt to associate the book with other writings accepted by the Jewish community. Josephus, as we observed above, was ready enough to use it in company with Ezra and Esther, though denying it the standing of Scripture.

Unfortunately, no Hebrew text of 1 Maccabees exists. It is unlikely that one would have been preserved at Qumran, where the Hasmonaeans were not popular, and the destruction of Jerusalem in 70 CE by the Romans probably meant the loss of most archival material from the temple and palace buildings. Our knowledge of the original author and his work will have to come from our reading of the present Greek text.

Further Reading

On the Apocrypha and its Writings

G.W.E. Nickelsburg, *Jewish Literature between the Bible and the Mishnah* (Philadelphia: Fortress Press, 1981). A useful introduction.

R.H. Pfeiffer, *A History of New Testament Times with an Introduction to the Apocrypha* (New York: Harper, 1949). This introduction, though dated, is still useful for its wealth of detailed information and assessment of earlier scholarship.

M.E. Stone (ed.), *Jewish Writings of the Second Temple Period* (Compendia Rerum Iudaicarum ad Novum Testamentum, 2.1; Assen: Van Gorcum; Philadelphia: Fortress Press, 1984). This joint Jewish and Christian work embodies the results of modern scholarly discussion of those ancient Jewish writings that are not to be found in either the Hebrew scriptures or the rabbinic collections. See especially Chapter 4, 'Historiography', by H.W. Attridge.

R.A. Kraft and G.W.E. Nickelsburg (eds.), *Early Judaism and its Modern Interpreters* (Atlanta: Scholars Press, 1986). A useful introduction to modern scholarship on many fields of early Judaism; see H.W. Attridge on 'Jewish Historiography', pp. 311-43, with a section on 'The Maccabean Histories'.

On the Greek Text and Manuscripts of 1 Maccabees

H.B. Swete, *Introduction to the Old Testament in Greek* (Cambridge: Cambridge University Press, 2nd edn, 1902). This classic introduction is a starting point for all scholars.

F.-M. Abel, *Les livres des Maccabées* (Paris: Gabalda, 1949). See Chapter 6, pp. liii-lix for invaluable details of the Greek, Latin, Syriac and other translations of 1 Maccabees.

F. Kenyon, *The Text of the Greek Bible* (London: Duckworth, 2nd edn, 1949). A very useful and practical general introduction to manuscripts, versions and texts of the Greek Bible.

On the Original Hebrew Version:

C.C. Torrey, 'Maccabees (Books)', in T.K. Cheyne (ed.), *Encyclopaedia Biblica* (London, 1902), III, cols. 2858-59.

2

THE COMPOSITION OF 1 MACCABEES

Signs of Composition

Having ascertained the history of the text of 1 Maccabees, we may now turn to consider the contents of the book. It is stating the obvious to say that the first thing any student of the book should do is to read it from beginning to end, preferably at one sitting, but it is surprising how few scholars ever do this. A careful reading will show us something of the contents and structure of the book, and so give us some clues to the author's intentions. The first major question that arises is whether the text as it has come to us is as it left the author's hands; has anything been added, or lost, from the original work? There are no obvious signs of loss, either in the manuscript evidence or in the continuity of the work. There are some signs of addition, but it seems most likely that these witness to the editorial work of the author rather than to the hand of a later interpolator. For example, chs. 14–16 have sometimes been seen as an addition, mainly on the grounds that Josephus had not used them. However, it is not certain that Josephus was ignorant of these chapters even if he did not use them, and there are no grounds from text, style or content for supposing that chs. 14–16 were not written by the author who composed chs. 1–13.

There are some passages that do not link smoothly into the surrounding text: thus ch. 5, about Judas's attacks on the surrounding Gentiles, appears to separate ch. 4 and ch. 6, and ch. 8, about the Romans, appears to intrude between the death of Nicanor (7.39-50) and Demetrius's intelligence of it (9.1); 12.1-23, about Jonathan's diplomatic relationships with Rome and Sparta, interrupts the story of his battles with Demetrius (11.63-74; 12.24-32.), and 15.15-24, about a Jewish diplomatic mission to Rome, has long been suspected of being misplaced, perhaps belonging after 14.24, following which 14.25-49, the encomium of Simon's achievements, also appears to form a similar 'island' in the text. But these 'island' sections (all incorporating documents) are probably to be interpreted as evidence of the author's compositional activity as he tried to integrate separate accounts of the Maccabees' activities at home and abroad into an intelligible sequence.

The book cites various other external documents (5.10-13; 8.23-32; 10.18-20; 10. 25b-45; 11.30-37; 12.6-18; 12.20-23; 13.36-40; 14.20-23; 14.27b-49; 15.2b-9; 15.16-21), but these, whether authentic or not (some scholars doubt the authenticity of the letters of Demetrius [10.25b-45] and Arius of Sparta [12.20-23]), were almost certainly incorporated from the first by the author, and are integral to the text, though some scholars have identified 8.23-30 (the Roman letter to the Jews) and 15.16-21 (the letter from Consul Lucius to King Ptolemy) as later insertions. A number of passages have been identified as poetic compositions on grounds of word-order and poetic parallelism (1.25-28; 1.36-40; 2.7b-13; 2.49d-68; 3.3-9a; 3.45; 3.50b-53; 4.30d-33; 4.38; 7.17; 9.21; 9.41; 14.4-15; the NRSV does not allow 2.49d-68 or 9.41, but adds 7.37-38), but apart from obvious quotations such as 9.21, this material also probably came from the hand and inspiration of the author, composing in traditional Hebrew style.

The Author's Use of Sources

There have been several attempts to discover signs of the use of earlier sources by the author of 1 Maccabees. In a dissertation published in 1954, K.-D. Schunk argued for the use of (i) a Seleucid court chronicle narrating and dating the reigns of official Seleucid rulers up to Antiochus VII; (ii) a Mattathias legend source (for parts of ch. 2); (iii) a Judas source (for chs. 1–9) (does 9.22 imply that the more important of Judas's deeds had been recorded?); (iv) a Jonathan source (for parts of ch. 12); (v) a Simon source (for parts of chs. 13–16); (vi) official yearbooks of the High-Priest, available for the high-priestly reigns of Jonathan and Simon; (vii) a Jewish state archival source, perhaps from Simon's time, from which the author drew most of the documents he quotes; cf. 14.49, which refers to copies of documents deposited in the 'treasury'. This final source is the most certain of these possibilities.

The existence of offical high-priestly records is possible, and they might be the source of the dates (given in years and months) preserved in 9.54 (death of Alcimus), 10.21 (Jonathan's vesting as high-priest), 13.51 (the Jewish re-entry to the citadel), 16.14 (Simon's final, fatal visit to Jericho). There is little if any internal evidence in the individual paragraphs credited to the alleged Simon or Jonathan sources to indicate that they ever had a common source. The possibility of a source telling of Judas's activities is attractive, for the author of 1 Maccabees was probably separated by half a century or more from the days of Judas, who died in 160 BCE; the most likely candidate is a source containing an account of Judas's campaigns against a series of Seleucid generals, into which other material (e.g. various poetic pieces, information of Seleucid activities, various campaigns by Judas and others in surrounding countries, an account of the temple rededication, and the diplomatic mission to Rome) has been interwoven.

The identification of a Seleucid chronicle depends on the isolation in 1 Maccabees of material using official Seleucid dating in a context of Seleucid (not Jewish) events (Schunk argues that Seleucid dates appear only in a Syrian context, but G.O. Neuhaus disputes this). If the author were using a Seleucid chronicle, one might expect to find more traces of the standard phraseology or formulae used in such compilations (as in the Deuteronomistic History, or the Seleucid kinglist published by Sachs and Wiseman, for example). One might also find traces of a pro-Seleucid bias remaining in the material used, in spite of editing. The use of such a Seleucid chronicle remains unproved. The origin of the material about Mattathias in ch. 2 is far from clear; most of it is probably the author's own composition, but the opening information in 2.1-5 is not exactly consistent with the author's presentation of the Maccabaean family in chs. 3–16 (where John is unmentioned, and Simon, Judas and Jonathan appear in a different order), and may be drawn from some archival source.

The Structure of 1 Maccabees

An examination of the structure of the book shows clear signs of deliberate arrangement and composition. Even on a casual reading through, it can immediately be seen that chs. 1–2 are an introduction to the book. Chapters 3.1–9.22 form a clearly defined section on the achievements of Judas; the opening and closing are clearly signalled. The final sentence of this section (9.22) is obviously modelled on sentences ending the accounts of the kings of Israel and Judah in 1 and 2 Kings. Chapters 9.23–12.52 describe the activities of Jonathan, and 12.53–16.23 tell of the achievements of Simon and his son John. Simon hands over to John at 16.3, and the book ends with a closure similar to that of 9.22, but this time referring to John. The achievements of Jonathan, Simon and John appear to belong together—there is no simple segmentation of their deeds in the narrative; their activities seem to overlap—and it may be that we should see the book as divided into Introduction (chs. 1–2), the achievements of Judas (3.1–9.22), and the work of Jonathan, Simon and John taken together, with clear emphasis on the central role of Simon. This would fit with the reference of Mattathias in 2.65-66 to the roles of Simon and Judas respectively, with no reference at that point to either Jonathan or John. The final words of the book, however, show that the author focuses at the end on the reign of John Hyrcanus, which marks the end of the Maccabaean rebellion; from this point, the Hasmonaean kingdom will be different.

Chapters 1–2: Introduction
Within these three major blocks of material, more detailed analysis of the structure is possible. Chapters 1 and 2 clearly form an introduction, in which the new situation created by Alexander the Great and his successors (in particular, the Selecuid king Antiochus IV) is countered by the response of the Israelite priest Mattathias. The book begins with a prologue (1.1-10) which sets the scene by recalling the division of Alexander's empire among his dynastic successors, the 'Diadochoi'. These founded separate kingdoms based in Greece and Macedonia (Cassander), Thrace (Lysimachus), Asia Minor (Antigonus), Babylonia (Seleucus), and Egypt (Ptolemy); the author of 1 Maccabees was concerned mainly with the Ptolemaic and Seleucid kingdoms between which Judah lay.

Chapter 1.11-64 describes the situation of apostasy into which the people of Israel fell under the Seleucids. The fault lay initially with certain Israelite renegades (1.11), whose policies (1.11-15) led to a series of disasters visited upon Israel by Antiochus—an attack on the Jewish temple (1.20-24), the destruction and subsequent garrisoning of Jerusalem (1.29-35), and finally the horrendous attack on the Jewish religion itself (1.41-64). The chapter is carefully constructed; the account of each attack is followed by a poetic lament (1.24-28; 1.36-40), the climactic attack receiving its lament from the mouth of Mattathias (2.7-13). The author makes it clear that he blames both the Jewish renegades (1.11-15) and the 'sinful root' (1.10), Antiochus IV himself, for these disasters, but he is repeatedly critical of the Jewish apostates (1.43, 52). Chapter 2 continues this theme and presents Jewish responses to this situation: that of the Jew who is ready to apostatise (2.23), that of the many who sought righteousness and peace but evaded the issue by withdrawing to the wilderness (2.29-38), and that of Mattathias the priest and the Hasidaeans (2.42-48) who met the problem head on and went to war . This is clearly presented as the correct response in the circumstances. This chapter is thus also carefully structured: Mattathias's personal action is contrasted with that of the Jewish apostate (2.15-26); those who sought righteousness and justice and withdrew are contrasted with the Hasidaeans, the mighty warriors of Israel, all who offered themselves willingly for the law (2.29-38; 42-48); and Mattathias's opening speech about not abandoning the religion and covenant of one's ancestors is echoed in his death-bed speech (2.51-58). The speech ends with Mattathias's commendation of his two sons, Simon as the counsellor of the Maccabaean movement and Judas as the warrior of it, which presages the basic division of the following chapters into two sections, one devoted to Judas and the other to Simon (see above).

Chapters 3.1–9.22: Judas
The first half of the narrative, 3.1–9.22, focuses on the achievements of Judas, and it is clearly a well-ordered structure in itself. It begins with an introduction to Judas and a poem in praise of him (3.1-9), and it ends at 9.19-22 with his burial and a short poetic lament over him. Within this framework, the narrative is divided into two similarly constructed halves, 3.10–6.63, ending with the Seleucid capture of the Maccabaean fortresses at Bethzur and Mount Zion, and 7.1–9.18, ending with the death of Judas in battle. In the first half, the chief actors are Judas, King Antiochus, and his generals Gorgias and Lysias; in the second half Judas, King Demetrius, and his generals Bacchides and Nicanor. The structure of the narrative and the sequence of events may be set out simply as follows:

A. 3.10-26   Two military attacks repulsed by Judas:
                        Apollonios (10-12) and Seron (13-26)
   3.27-37   Antiochus IV's response
   3.38–4.35   Two military attacks repulsed by Judas:
                        Gorgias (3.28–4.25) and Lysias (4.26-35)
   4.36-59   The cleansing of the sanctuary
   4.60-61   Judas's fortification of Mt Zion and Bethzur

   [5.1-68   Campaigns against the surrounding Gentiles]

   6.1-16   Antiochus IV's response and death
   6.17-63   Judas's attack on the Seleucid garrison in Jerusalem; the

The author has organized his material coherently. In both sections, A and B, Judas begins well, makes progress, but ends with a serious setback—a defeat (A), and death (B). In the first section, set in the reigns of Antiochus IV and V, Judas wins four engagements, over increasingly senior generals and more experienced forces, takes over the temple courts and purifies them, and fortifies Mt Zion and the town of Bethzur to the south; he even wins an offer of peace from the Seleucids, but the Seleucids regain control of Mt Zion and Bethzur. In the second section, set in the reign of Demetrius, Judas makes rule impossible for Alcimus, and defeats the general Nicanor in the battle of Capharsalama. Nicanor is killed at the battle of Adasa, but this success is counterbalanced by the death of Judas after the battle against Bacchides. The two sections thus follow a basically similar pattern. In each section, the author has incorporated a distinct block of material—in the first section, ch. 5, detailing Maccabaean campaigns against Gentiles in Idumaea, Ammon, Gilead, Galilee, the sea coast, and Philistia, and in the second section, ch. 8, describing the Roman government and giving an account of a diplomatic mission sent by Judas to Rome. These were difficult to integrate into the basic narrative, which was concerned primarily with Maccabaean military campaigns in Palestine against the Seleucid forces, and the author's method was simply to build in these separate blocks of material at the high points of Jewish success—after the rededication of the sanctuary in the first case and the defeat of Nicanor in the second.

Chapters 9.23–16.23: Jonathan and Simon
1 Maccabees 9.23–16.23 forms the third major part of the Maccabaean

history. The structure of the composition here seems much more complex, and events much more interwoven. Jonathan, Simon and his son John move in a world of Hellenistic intrigue, making and breaking alliances with Egypt, Syria, Rome and Sparta. There are more diplomatic letters than poetic laments, more politics than religion. The structure of the narrative and the sequence of events are not easy to present simply and clearly, and one senses that the author himself felt this. Thus, for example, the break between the leadership of Judas and the leadership of Jonathan is clear (cf. 9.22, 23, 29), but it happens within the context of the campaigns of Bacchides (9.1-73), and the real turning point appears to come when Bacchides agrees to terms of peace, departs from Israel, and Jonathan began to judge the people (9.73). In the following chapters, the narrative zig-zags as it presents Jonathan's diplomatic dealings with Alexander, Demetrius, Ptolemy and Trypho; the story of Jonathan's war with Demetrius II is broken to allow the insertion of dealings with Rome and Sparta in 12.1-23. An equal lack of integration is clear in the narrative of subsequent dealings with Rome and Sparta in 14.16-24. The takeover from Jonathan by Simon is not clear-cut (see 12.48, 49-53; 13.8, 14, 19, 23), and the death of Simon (drunk, 16.16) is an anticlimax after his political achievements; the book ends with a reference to his son John's accession as high-priest.

This complex narrative might be outlined as follows, though the detailed analysis of the compositional blocks, their definition and their interconnection, is open to debate:

9.23-73	Alcimus dies, Bacchides grants peace, Jonathan becomes leader.
10.1-50	Alexander Balas and Demetrius I vie for Jonathan's support; Jonathan rejects Demetrius, Alexander defeats Demetrius.
10.51-66	Alexander allies with Ptolemy and honours Jonathan.
10.67-89	Demetrius II arrives: Jonathan defeats his army.
11.1-19	Ptolemy and Alexander die in power stuggle; Demetrius II is left supreme.
11.20-37, 38-53	Jonathan's relationships with Demetrius.
11.54-59	Trypho and Antiochus VI offer positions to Jonathan and Simon.
11.60-74	Jonathan accepts homage of Askalon, takes Gaza; Simon takes Bethzur; Jonathan defeats Demetrius's army.

[12.1-23	Jonathan renews friendship with Rome and allies with ` Sparta.]
12.24-38	Jonathan defeats Demetrius's force; Simon and Jonathan take Joppa, fortify Jerusalem and Adida.
12.39–13.32	Trypho seizes power, captures and kills Jonathan and King Antiochus.
13.33-53	Simon's success.
14.1-3	Demetrius II's campaign in Media; his capture.
14.4-15	Poem in praise of Simon.

This seems to form a natural ending to the book, the poem about Simon's achievements in 14.4-15 balancing the poem celebrating Judas's achievements in 3.3-9, and at one stage of his composition the author may indeed have intended this as the end. However, he clearly wished to add the long, eulogistic public record of the achievements of Simon, apparently copied from bronze tablets set up on Mt Zion (14.25-49), and he had further material, some of it also from bronze tablets, about Simon's relations with Rome and Sparta (14.16-24), which has often been seen as awkwardly placed at this point. The author had also at his disposal an account of Simon's dealings with Antiochus VII, and the subsequent campaign; this is linked back to Simon's occupation of Gazara, where Simon's son John was stationed (13.53), by reference to John in 16.1. Finally, it was natural to add an account of the death of Simon and a short conclusion referring to the deeds of Simon's son John Hyrcanus (16.23-24). The final sections of the book are as follows:

[14.16-24	Bronze tablets from Rome, letter from Sparta; mission to Rome.]
[14.25-49	Decree on bronze tablets about Simon.]
15.1-9	Letter of Antiochus VII to Simon.
15.10-14	Antiochus VII besieges Trypho in Dor.
[15.15-24	Letters from Rome to kings and countries (cf. 14.24).]
15.25-36	Antiochus VII's dispute with Simon.
15.37–16.10	Cendebeus's invasion of Judaea.
16.11-22	Death of Simon.
16.23-24	Author's conclusion.

The Author's Concerns and Theological Standpoint
With this analysis of the book in front of us, it is now possible to see the author's main concerns, and to sketch his theological principles. It is immediately clear that the author is concerned above all about Israel's relationship with the peoples that surrounded it, both politically and

religiously. His narrative deals with Maccabaean relationships with the Seleucid Empire, the Ptolemaic Empire, the developing Roman Empire, the cities of the Mediterranean coast to the west and the peoples of Transjordan to the east. Politically, the author looks for Israel's independence of other nations and empires. The aim of Judas and Simon is to free Israel from their domination. He accepts the need of of diplomatic negotiations, and appears even to be proud of the Maccabees' diplomatic successes with Rome and Sparta, because they tend to establish Israel's autonomy, even if they commit the Maccabees to offering military aid in certain circumstances. At another level, however, the author sees the nations as the cause of all evil, and their influence on Israel to be passionately resisted. The first paragraph after the prologue says it all:

> In those days certain renegades came out from Israel and misled many, saying, 'Let us go and make a covenant with the Gentiles around us, for since we separated from them many disasters have come upon us.' This proposal pleased them, and some of the people eagerly went to the king, who authorized them to observe the ordinances of the Gentiles. So they built a gymnasium in Jerusalem, according to Gentile custom, and removed the marks of circumcision, and abandoned the holy covenant. They joined with the Gentiles and sold themselves to do evil (1.11-15).

The author has great contempt for renegade Jews, who join foreign armies (3.15), appeal to the Seleucid king (6.21-27), oppose Judas (7.5-7), and delate Jonathan to Alexander (10.61; 11.21), but expresses fierce anger against foreign enemies who are in fact the enemies of God (cf. Schwartz, *JJS* 42 [1991], pp.16-38). Their wickedness is signalled in the opening verses by the comment that Alexander the Great, who founded the Hellenistic kingdoms, 'was exalted, and his heart was lifted up' (1.3); Antiochus IV was 'a sinful root' (1.10), whose decree was intended to make Israel 'forget the law' (1.49); Mattathias and his friends 'rescued the law out of the hands of the Gentiles and kings, and they never let the sinner gain the upper hand' (2.48); Mattathias instructed his followers, 'Pay back the Gentiles in full, and heed what the law commands' (2.68). In 5.1-2, the Gentiles, hearing that the altar had been rebuilt and the sanctuary rededicated, 'determined to destroy the descendants of Jacob who lived among them'. 'They come against us in great pride and lawlessness to destroy us and our wives and our children, and to despoil us; but we fight for our lives and our laws. He himself [i.e. God] will crush them before us', says Judas before battle against the Seleucid army (3.20). 'Be ready...to fight with these Gentiles who have assembled against us to destroy us and our sanctuary' (3.59).

This identification of foreign enemies as those determined to destroy the law and the sanctuary is the mainspring of the author's plot. The Israelites, and in particular the Maccabees, are those who keep, or who should keep, the law and who defend the sanctuary; thus Simon encourages the people by saying, 'You yourselves know what great things I and my brothers and the house of my father have done for the laws and the sanctuary' (13.3). The author describes the Maccabees as 'the family of those men through whom deliverance was given to Israel' (5.62), and the structure and contents of his book quite clearly emphasize the part played by that family (especially Judas and Simon) in rescuing Israel from her enemies and establishing peace in the land (14.11). It has been argued, on the grounds that 14.4-48 and 15.15-24 are not an original part of the book, that the author is less approving of Simon than is usually thought, but, even if we ignore these passages, there remains the evidence of Simon's achievements in chs. 12 and 13 and the poem of 14.3-15. It is less certain, however, that (as some argue) the author is giving political support to any of the successors of Simon; 'the rest of the acts of John' are mentioned only summarily (16.23), and the author clearly has no intention of recounting them, whether for praise or blame.

There are many indications of the author's general theological standpoint. He prefers, probably out of respect, to speak of 'heaven' rather than of 'the God of heaven' (e.g. 3.18; 16.3). He knows that none who trust in God will lack strength (1.61), and that it is God who gives victory to the Maccabees (3.18-22). Israelites are to follow the examples of the earlier heroes of the faith—Abraham, Joseph, Phinehas, Joshua, Caleb, David, Elijah, Hananiah, Azariah and Mishael, and Daniel (the author's reading therefore extends beyond the law and the prophets). Prayer, fasting, and enquiry of the law, the offering of tithes and first fruits, and the dedication of the Nazirites are all important (3.44-49), as are the observance of sabbaths and feasts, sabbatical years, circumcision, the laws of cleanliness, the offering of daily sacrifices in the sanctuary, and the partition of the outer and inner courts in the sanctuary (cf. 9.54-55). Idols and idolaters alike are to be destroyed (cf. 10.84). The author's acceptance of these practices suggests that he was traditional in his religious attitudes, and that the performance of religion was part of his nationalism. A threat to the temple was a threat to the nation.

More interestingly, the author, for all his support of the Maccabees as deliverers of Israel, does not suggest that they fulfil any messianic prophecies or owe anything to the house of David. David is mentioned once, in 2.57, as an example to be followed: 'because he was merciful, [he] inherited the throne of the kingdom for ever'. The Maccabees are successful deliverers of Israel, not as messianic figures but through the strength of their faith in the Torah. The troubles that have come upon Israel are not punishment for Israel's earlier, pre-exilic sins, as so often in the prophetic books, but the result of present apostasy by those who wished to consort with the Gentiles (1.11). Antiochus IV is a 'sinful root', but his sin is not pride, as in Daniel and 2 Maccabees, but rather his error of judgment in attacking Jerusalem and the law (6.8-13 portrays the king more sympathetically than 2 Macc. 9 or Dan. 7.20, 25; 8.9-14, 23-25; 9.27; 11.21-45). The author of 1 Maccabees (unlike the author of 2 Maccabees) saw no sense or glory in martyrdom (defence was approved if the enemy attacked on the sabbath: 2.29-41; 9.43-49), had no expectation of resurrection (contrast 2 Macc. 7; 12.43-45; and Dan. 12.2), and did not expect success to come through the sort of dramatic miracles described in 2 Maccabees. Israel's hope lay in the Maccabaean establishment of independence, peace and fruitfulness in the land, coupled with the improved glory of the sanctuary (14.3-15). That Judas and Jonathan died before this hope was realized is not explained, but great lamentation is made for them by Israel, and an imposing family tomb is built (9.19-21; 13.27-30) as a memorial to the Maccabaean family.

   The author's attitude to Scripture, and especially to prophecy, is important. He clearly knows the five books of the Law and refers among other things to the stories of Abraham, Joseph and Phinehas (2.52-54), the Exodus (4.9), the covenant (1.15), the rules of the sabbatical year (6.49), the high-priestly vestments and the Feast of Tabernacles (10.21; cf. Exod. 28.1-39; Lev. 23.33-43), and the rules of war (3.56; cf. Deut. 20.5-8). The author knows the historical books well (Judges, Joshua, Samuel, Kings) and apparently takes them as his model (cf. 9.22; 9.73; 16.23), occasionally referring to them or even quoting from them (e.g., 2.57, cf. 2 Sam. 7.15f.; 6.41, cf. 2 Kgs 19.35; 9.21, cf. 2 Sam. 2.19). The priestly genealogy of Mattathias (14.29) is given in 1 Chron. 24.7-18; there are allusions to Ezra 6.8; 7.10, 20 in 1 Macc. 10.44 and 14.14 (royal payments for sanctuaries and walls, and Simon's concern for the law). The incorporation of archival documents may suggest that the author is also imitating the author of Ezra, and even that he intends to write a continuation of the Chronicler's history into his own time.

   The author's knowledge of the prophetic writings is less immediately obvious. There are some clear quotations, most obviously in the account of the death of Mattathias's son John (9.35-42), where v. 41 appears to quote Amos 8.10, or in the poem of 14.4-15, where v. 8-9 reflect Ezek. 34.27, Zech. 8.12, 8.4, and v. 12 reflects Mic. 4.4 and Zech. 3.10; G. Neuhaus, however, finds a total of no less than 115 citations and allusions, and argues that the author of 1 Maccabees understands the scriptures as prophecy, and the Maccabaean period as the time of their fulfilment, as in the passages just quoted. However, the author makes no attempt to connect the return of Jews to Judaea from life among the Gentiles in 5.23, 45, 53-54, or the establishment of independent rule in Judaea, with prophetic oracles predicting a Jewish return from the diaspora or a coming messianic kingdom. (The comparison of Judas with Saul's son Jonathan at 9.21, and the possible hints of David the warrior in 3.3 and Solomon the successful monarch in 14.4-15, are hardly enough to establish a 'messianic' understanding of Judas and Simon.) The author does not refer to biblical prophets by name, notes that prophets have ceased to appear in Israel (9.27), and refers to the expectation that there might be a future prophet to provide answers to difficult questions (4.46; 14.41; cf. Deut. 18.14; Mal. 4.5; Neh. 7.65; Jn 1.21 for a similar expectation). The author's attitude to prophecy seems ambiguous; he does not give it a major role in either past, present or future, yet he is undoubtedly aware of it.

In addition to the law and the prophets, the author is also very aware (probably from his experience of worship in the temple) of the Psalms, especially in the first half of the book. The laments of 1.25-28; 36-40; 2.7-13; 3.45-47 are reminiscent of Psalms 44, 74 and 79, and the Lamentations of Jeremiah. Chapter 2.63 perhaps alludes to Ps. 37.10, 35-36, ch. 4.24 quotes the opening verse of Ps. 118 or Ps. 136, and 7.17 draws on Ps. 79.3.

The author has used the law, the prophets and the psalms to demonstrate the national and religious importance of the events of the Maccabaean revolution. The Maccabees by their actions continue the history of Israel, which has not yet reached its end or climax. For this author, there is more history to come, under the successors of John Hyrcanus. He probably knows the book of Daniel, as is suggested by the references to 'desolating sacrilege' erected on the altar of burnt offering (1.54; cf. Dan. 9.27; 11.31), to Hananiah, Azariah, Mishael and Daniel in 2.59-60 (cf. Dan. 1.7), though he never mentions it by name and can hardly regard it as scriptural. J.A. Goldstein has argued that the author of 1 Maccabees consciously rejects Daniel's theological presentation of events; thus in 1 Maccabees Antiochus's persecution is not punishment for earlier sins of Israel (Dan. 9.1-19, 24), events do not happen in accordance with an apocalyptic timetable decreed by God (and indeed events continued beyond the several final dates predicted by Daniel), martyrdom is not acceptable, resurrection to reward or punishment is not expected, and the Maccabees are certainly more than 'a little help' (if that description in Dan. 11.34 refers to them, as is generally thought).

The Author of 1 Maccabees
All this invites the obvious questions about the background, date and identity of the author. His name is unknown, and will probably remain so, but we would have to look for him among the educated aristocracy of Jerusalem of the late second or early first century BCE. His first language was probably Hebrew, but he would have to understand Greek in order to use documents originating from Seleucid, Roman and Spartan chancelleries and translate them into Hebrew. He was clearly a Jew, well versed in the scriptures and the temple liturgy. He may have been a priest, but there is no sign in his book of particular sympathy for the priesthood. His instincts are political, and he might have been a courtier of John Hyrcanus or one of his earlier successors, writing for his political contemporaries. In either case, he had access to treasury and probably temple archives, and had sufficient income, leisure and resources to write his history. It is generally supposed that his allegiances would have been with the Sadducees rather than the Pharisees, on the grounds that he shows little sympathy for ideas related to apocalyptic speculation or life after death; if he were closely associated with Hyrcanus, he may well have chosen to avoid association with the Pharisees, who opposed Hyrcanus in his later years. He was clearly a loyal supporter of the Maccabaean family, and a convinced nationalist, but he was a man of intellectual integrity and reasonable scholarly objectivity who avoided demonizing the Seleucid enemy (his account of the death of Antiochus IV, 'ungodly' though he was [10.10], is much more sympathetic than that of 2 Maccabees [compare 1 Macc. 6.13-18 with 2 Macc. 9.1-28]). His writing is on the whole factual and objective, and perhaps in spite of the author's Maccabaean sympathies, owes something to Hellenistic historiography.

1 Maccabees is usually dated to the later years of the reign of John Hyrcanus (134–104 BCE), or to a period not too long after his death, on the grounds of the reference to the already recorded achievements

of Hyrcanus in 16.23-24, and the reference in 13.30 to the existence of the Maccabees' family tomb, built by Simon, 'to this day'. S. Schwartz thinks the book, with its hostility to the Gentiles roundabout, was written c. 130 BCE before Hyrcanus incopororated Idumaea and Samaria into the growing Hasmonaean kingdom, and A. Momigliano has similarly argued that the book was written between the death of Simon and 129 BCE, on the grounds that the information about the Romans in 1 Maccabees 8 fits best the period between the destruction of Corinth in 146 BCE (cf. 1 Macc. 8.9-10) and the incorporation of Pergamum into the Roman Empire between 133 and 130 BCE, on which 1 Maccabees 8 is surprisingly silent. However, 1 Macc. 8.2-16 is a separate piece about Roman government, composed by the author from hearsay (v. 2), and cannot be used to limit the writing of the whole book to a date pre-129 BCE, as Momigliano does. Further, the phrase 'to this day' (1 Macc. 8.10; 16.24), particularly in 16.24, is hardly justified by a date as early as 130 BCE—even if the writer is thinking (as Momigliano suggests) of future readers. A composition date in the last decade of the second or the first decade of the first century BCE remains most likely for 1 Maccabees. All are agreed that the book must have been written before Pompey captured Jerusalem and entered the temple in 63 BCE, for the work has no trace of hostility towards Rome.

Further Reading

On the Composition and Structure of 1 Maccabees

N. Martola, *Capture and Liberation: A Study in the Composition of the First Book of Maccabees* (Acta Academiae Aboensis, Ser. A, Humaniora, 63.1; Abo: Abo Akademi, 1984). This is the only detailed study of the subject. It demands concentration, but is carefully argued and rewarding.

On the Sources of 1 Maccabees

K-D. Schunk, *Die Quellen des I und II Makkabäerbuches* (Halle: Niemeyer, 1954). This important book should be read in conjunction with the reviews of it by J.C. Dancy, *JTS* NS 6 (1953), pp. 265-67, and F.V. Filson, *JBL* 75 (1956), p. 87, and the more detailed critique by G.O. Neuhaus, 'Quellen um 1 Makkabaerbuch?', *JSJ* 5 (1974), pp. 162-75.

J.A. Goldstein, *1 Maccabees* (Anchor Bible, 41; Garden City, NY: Doubleday), pp. 37-54, 90-103, and *2 Maccabees* (Anchor Bible, 41A; Garden City, NY: Doubleday), pp. 28-54. In *1 Maccabees* Goldstein argues that 1 Maccabees probably knew the *Testament of Moses*, possibly contains a faint allusion to 1 Enoch 85–90, and 'seems to take a delight in proving the oracles of Daniel false' (p. 45). 1 Maccabees used documents, oral tradition and a supposed work on the deaths of persecutors. In 2

Maccabees, Goldstein argues that in addition 1 and 2 Maccabees used a common Jewish source, possibly written by Eupolemos before 130 BCE. The last two hypothetical sources may be accepted only with caution.

On Poetry in 1 Maccabees

G.O. Neuhaus, *Studien zu den poetischen Stücken im 1 Makkabäerbuch* (Würzburg: Echter-Verlag, 1974).

N. Martola, *Capture and Liberation: A Study in the Composition of the First Book of Maccabees* (Abo: Abo Akademi, 1984), pp. 36-56.

On the Author's Theological and Historical Concerns

D. Arenhoevel, 'Die Eschatologie der Makkabäerbucher', *TTZ* 72 (1963), pp. 257-69.

D. Arenhoevel, *Die Theokratie nach dem 1. und 2. Makkabäerbuch* (Walberger Studien, 3; Mainz: Grünewald, 1967).

H.W. Attridge, 'Jewish Historiography', in R.A. Kraft and G.W.E. Nickelsburg (eds.), Early Judaism and its Modern Interpreters (Atlanta: Scholars Press, 1986), pp. 311-43.

R.H. Pfeiffer, *A History of New Testament Times* (New York: Harper, 1949), pp. 491-96.

B. Renaud, 'Le Loi et les lois dans les livres des Maccabees', *RB* 68 (1961), pp. 39-67.

S. Schwartz, 'Israel and the Nations Roundabout: 1 Maccabees and the Hasmonaean Expansion', *JJS* 42 (1991), pp. 16-38.

On the Date of 1 Maccabees

In addition to the commentaries, see

A. Momigliano, 'The Date of the 1st Book of Maccabees', pp. 561-66 in *Sesto contributi alla storia degli studi classici e del mondo antico*, II (Roma: Storia & Letteratura 150, 1980).

S. Schwartz, 'Israel and the Nations Roundabout: 1 Maccabees and Hasmonaean Expansion', *JJS* 42 (1991), pp. 16-38.

3

CHRONOLOGY AND SEQUENCE

The Problems of Dating

1 Maccabees describes how in the forty and more years from 176 to 134 BCE the Jews, through much suffering, established their religious and political independence from Seleucid control under the leadership of the Maccabaean family. The author of 1 Maccabees has told the story in a relatively factual and precise way, dating events with considerable care. Many of the dates are given with reference to a particular year of 'the kingdom of the Greeks' (1.10), and the starting point for this chronology was the foundation of the Seleucid era by its first ruler, Seleucus I. Seleucus dated his reign from his conquest of Babylon in the sixth year of Alexander IV, the son of Alexander the Great (see E.J. Bickerman, *Chronology of the Ancient World*, revised edn, 1980, p. 71). By our calendar, that year may be dated April 312–April 311 BCE. But this left an awkward legacy in that, while Babylon and the eastern part of the Empire began its calendar year in the spring with the month Nisan (approximately April), Macedonia and the western part of the Seleucid Empire began their year in the autumn (in Jewish and Semitic terms, with the month Tishri, approximately October). The Seleucid era, thus, might be counted in the west from autumn 312 BCE (this is the usage of, e.g., 1 Macc. 6.16, which dates Antiochus IV's death to Seleucid year 149), and in the east from either spring 312 BCE or from spring 311 BCE (this latter is the usage of the Hellenistic Babylonian kinglist recording the death of Antiochus IV in Seleucid year 148, published by Sachs and Wiseman). In Julian terms, then, the 150th year of the era, which falls within our period (see 1 Macc. 6.20), might run from spring 163 BCE, from autumn 163 BCE or from spring 162 BCE, depending on which system we believe the author to be using at this point. As it is possible that the author of 1 Maccabees was compiling his material from two different sources, one of which perhaps used an

autumnal and the other a spring system, there is room for debate about the precise dating of a number of events; and a decision about one date will have consequences for the determination of other dates.

It has often been suggested (originally by E.J. Bickerman) that the author of 1 Maccabees used a royal Seleucid chronicle, with dates based on the Macedonian era dating from autumn 312 BCE, for the dating of political events, and a Jewish source, perhaps temple archives or high-priestly lists, using a spring new year, to date events of religious concern. 1 Macc. 10.21, for example, notes that Jonathan put on the high-priestly garments in the seventh month of the 160th year, at the Feast of Tabernacles. The reference to the feast in the seventh month suggests a spring dating and a Jewish background. (The identification of autumnal and vernal dates has in turn been used as evidence for the distinction of sources in 1 Maccabees.) The picture is even further complicated by the fact that 1 and 2 Maccabees disagree about the sequence and dating of several important events (e.g. the death of Antiochus IV, and the campaigns of Lysias relative to the rededication of the temple). A vast scholarly literature has developed on this problem and its many ramifications.

Dates in 1 Maccabees

In order to disentangle this particular complexity as far as possible, we will begin by listing the dates given by 1 Maccabees, and then we will show in a chart where each would fall if calculated from spring 312 BCE, autumn 312 BCE or spring 311 BCE. This will indicate internal difficulties or inconsistencies of the book's dating, but it will also demonstrate that in a number of cases a particular event, whether dated by the autumn 312 or the spring 311 BCE system, will nevertheless fall in the same Julian year. The particular problems of a few dates may then be discussed.

1.10	137th year★	Accession of Antiochus IV
1.20	143rd year.★	Antiochus returns from Egypt, enters Jerusalem temple
1.29	'two years later' [i.e. 144th year]	Plundering of temple; building of citadel
1.54	15th Chislev, 145th year	Desecration of temple and persecution
1.59	25th Chislev [145th year]	Offering of sacrifice on sacrilegious altar
2.70	146th year	Death of Mattathias
3.37	147th year★	Departure of Antiochus for upper provinces

4.28	'the next year' [148th year]	Lysias's campaign into Idumaea
4.52	25th day, 9th month, 148th year	Dedication of new altar
6.16	149th year★	Death of Antiochus IV
6.20	150th year	Judas's siege of citadel
7.1	151st year★	Demetrius's accession; death of Lysias and Antiochus V
7.43	13th Adar [151st year]	Death of Nicanor
9.3	1st month, 152nd year	Bacchides's invasion; death of Judas
9.54	2nd month, 153rd year	Death of Alcimus
10.1	160th year★	Alexander Balas begins to reign
10.21	7th month, 160th year	Jonathan puts on sacred vestments
10.57	162nd year★	Alexander Balas marries Ptolemy's daughter
10.67	167th year★	Demetrius II returns from Crete to Syria
11.19	167th year★	Death of Alexander and Ptolemy; Demetrius II takes throne
13.41	170th year★	'Yoke of Gentiles removed'; first year of Simon
13.51	23rd day, 2nd month, 171st year	Jews entered citadel with rejoicing
14.1	172nd year★	Demetrius II invades Media; is captured
14.27	18th day of Elul, 172nd year	Third year of Simon, proclamation
15.10	174th year★	Antiochus VII Sidetes invades Syria
16.14	11th month Shebat, 177th year	Death of Simon at Jericho

The dates asterisked are credited by K.-D. Schunk to a Seleucid source, the remainder to a Jewish source. Dates with Jewish month names attached (1.54, 59; 7.43; 14.27; 16.14) may derive from a Jewish source, as might also, on grounds of content, 1.29; 2.70; 4.52; 9.54; 10.21; 13.41; 13.51. Several dates, at least on grounds of form, might come from either source (4.28; 6.20; 9.3). A glance at this list shows that the author is writing a carefully sequenced work; all dates given are in chronological order, and difficulties (notably with 6.20 and 10.1, 21) are few. However, owing to the possibility of the use of different eras already noted, the translation of these dates into Julian dates is sometimes a matter of debate.

The following table demonstrates the relationship of the years of the three possible Seleucid eras: Seleucid Babylonian era beginning spring 312 BCE; Seleucid Macedonian era beginning autumn 312 BCE; Seleucid Babylonian era beginning spring 311 BCE. If we follow the Babylonian era beginning in 312 BCE, events occur one year earlier by the Julian calendar than they do if we follow the spring 311 era.

The table assumes that the author of 1 Maccabees has its dated events in the correct *sequence*, and that it follows the Seleucid Babylonian era beginning in spring 312 BCE for all 'Jewish' dates, and the Macedonian Babylonian era beginning in autumn 312 BCE for all 'Seleucid' dates. (N.B. This is not a complete chart of events, but a chart of dates given by 1 Maccabees; years for which no dates are given are omitted.)

Date (BCE)	Sel. Bab. (Nisan 312)	Sel. Mac. (Tishri 312)	Sel. Bab. (Nisan 311)	Ref. (1 Macc.)	Year (Sel.)	Event (1 Macc.)
176						
Spring	137		136			
Autumn		137		1.10	137★	Accession of Antiochus IV (Sept. 175 BCE)
170						
Spring	143		142			
Autumn		143		1.20	143★	Antiochus returns from Egypt, enters Jerusalem temple (169 BCE)
169						
Spring	144		143			
Autumn		144		1.29	'2 years later' [i.e. 144]★	Plundering of Jerusalem; building of citadel (168 BCE)
168						
Spring	145		144	1.54	145	15th Chislev, desecration of temple (on Sel. Bab. or Sel. Macc. 312 era Dec. 168 BCE)
Autumn		145				

Date (BCE)	Sel. Bab. (Nisan 312)	Sel. Mac. (Tishri 312)	Sel. Bab. (Nisan 311)	Ref. (1 Macc.)	Year (Sel.)	Event (1 Macc.)
167						
Spring	146		145	2.70	146	Death of
Autumn		146				Mattathias
166						
Spring	147		146			
Autumn		147		3.37	147★	Departure of Antiochus for upper provinces
165						
Spring	148		147			
Autumn		148		4.28	['the next year', i.e. 148] 148★	Lysias's campaign into Idumaea
				4.52	148	25th day, 9th month, dedication of new altar (on Sel. Bab. 312 era, Dec. 165 BCE)
164						
Spring	149		148			
Autumn		149		6.16	149★	Death of Antiochus IV (Nov/Dec. 164 BCE)
163						
Spring	150		149	6.20	150	Judas's siege of citadel (spring–summer; Sel. Bab. 312 era)
Autumn		150		6.20	150★	Judas's siege of citadel (late autumn, Sel. Macc. 312 era)
162						
Spring	151		150			
Autumn		151		7.1	151★	Demetrius's accession; death of Lysias and Antiochus V.

Date (BCE)	Sel. Bab. (Nisan 312)	Sel. Mac. (Tishri 312)	Sel. Bab. (Nisan 311)	Ref. (1 Macc.)	Year (Sel.)	Event (1 Macc.)
161						
Spring	152		151	7.43	13 Adar [151]	Death of Nicanor (March 161)
				9.3	1st month 152	Bacchides's invasion, death of Judas, spring 161 BCE
Autumn		152				
160						
Spring	153		152	9.54	2nd month 153	Death of Alcimus
Autumn		153				
....						
153						
Spring	160		159			
Autumn		160		10.1	160★	Balas begins reign
				10.21	160, 7th month	Jonathan puts on vestments
152						
Spring	161		160			
Autumn		161				
151						
Spring	162		161			
		162		10.57	162★	Balas's wedding
148						
Spring	165		164			
Autumn		165		10.67	165★	Demetrius II returns to Syria
146						
Spring	167		166			
Autumn		167		11.19	167★	Deaths of Alexander and Ptolemy; Demetrius II reigns

Date (BCE)	Sel. Bab. (Nisan 312)	Sel. Mac. (Tishri 312)	Sel. Bab. (Nisan 311)	Ref. (1 Macc.)	Year (Sel.)	Event (1 Macc.)
143						
Spring	170		169	13.41	170	Gentile yoke removed;
Autumn		170				Simon's 1st year
142						
Spring	171		170	13.51	171, 23rd day, 2nd month	Jews enter citadel, rejoicing
Autumn		171				
141						
Spring	172		171			
Autumn		172		14.1	172★	Demetrius II invades Media
				14.27	172 18th Elul, day	Simon's 3rd year, proclamation
140						
Spring	173		172	14.27		
Autumn		173				
139						
Spring	174		173			
Autumn		174		15.10★	174	Antiochus VII invades Syria
136						
Spring	177		176	16.14	177, 11th mth	Shebat, death of Simon at Jericho, early 135 BCE
Autumn		177				
135						
Spring	176		177			
Autumn		176				

The sequence given above, which uses a Seleucid Babylonian era dating from spring 312 BCE for all 'Jewish' dates (i.e. those dates that do not derive from an official Seleucid source using an era from autumn 312 BCE) offers certain advantages, but also certain difficulties.

(i) If we accept a Seleucid Babylonian spring 312 era for the dates given in 1 Macc. 1.54 and 4.52, the desecration of the temple and the dedication of the new altar three years later may be dated to December 168 and December 165 BCE respectively. This allows for time between Judas's recapture of the temple area and the death of Antiochus IV between 19/20 November and 18/19 December 164 BCE. If, on the usual supposition of a Seleucid Babylonian spring 311 BCE era, the dedication of the new altar does not take place until December 164 BCE, there is no time for Antiochus to hear of it and other Jewish successes before his death, as recorded in 1 Macc. 6.5-7.

(ii) According to 1 Macc. 6.16, Antiochus died in the year Seleucid Macedonia 149 (which ran from autumn 164 BCE). According to 1 Macc. 6.20, in the year 150 Judas besieged the citadel in Jerusalem. If the date 150 in 1 Macc. 6.20 is also based on the Seleucid autumn era, it would refer to some time after autumn 163 BCE, perhaps even summer 162 BCE, which is far too late; if we can refer the date to the Seleucid Babylonian era from spring 312 BCE, we can date the attack on the citadel to summer 163 BCE, which seems correct. Most scholars agree that here 1 Maccabees is reckoning with a spring 312 BCE era, but the style of the date suggests rather an autumn 312 era dating; this could just be possible if Judas attacked the citadel in autumn 163 BCE, at the very beginning of the year.

(iii) The Seleucid Babylonian spring era from 312 BCE fits well also for the date in 9.3, the invasion of Bacchides in the first month of the year 152; this would be in early spring of 161 BCE, shortly after the death of Nicanor on 13 Adar at the end of the preceding year Seleucid 151. This would bring the death of Judas to spring 161 BCE; most scholars, following the Seleucid Babylonian era from spring 311 BCE, would date this in spring 160 BCE.

(iv) The two dates that cause difficulties for all systems are 1 Macc. 10.1 and 21. According to 1 Macc. 10.1, Alexander Balas landed and occupied Ptolemais in the year 160 of the Seleucid era. If this date is based on the Seleucid Macedonian era from autumn 312 BCE, year 160 began in autumn 153 BCE. 1 Macc. 10.21 says that Jonathan, newly appointed high-priest by Balas (1 Macc. 10.18-21), put on the high-priestly garments in the seventh month of the 160th year, at the Feast of Tabernacles. If 1 Maccabees is using for this event a dating scheme based on the Seleucid Babylonian spring 312 BC era, Jonathan took up the highpriesthood publicly at Tabernacles 153 BCE, within a fortnight of Balas's arrival at Ptolemais. This is not actually impossible, but it seems unlikely. Many scholars therefore would prefer to use a date based on the Seleucid Babylonian spring 311 era for 1 Macc. 10.21, and have Jonathan take up the high-priesthood in autumn 152 BCE, Alexander Balas having landed at Ptolemais some time in summer 152 BCE (still within year 160 if that date is based on the autumn 312 era). Other scholars argue that both dates, in 1 Macc. 10.1 and 21, are based on the spring 312 BCE era, the year 160 thus covering spring 153-spring 152, Alexander arriving at Ptolemais in the summer of 153 and Jonathan becoming high-priest at Tabernacles in the autumn of the same year.

It must, however, be noted that a large number of scholars date 'Jewish' events in 1 Maccabees by reference to the Seleucid Babylonian era dating from spring 311 BCE. Given the evidence for this spring 311 era in the Babylonian kinglist, this is a perfectly reasonable thing to do. This naturally has the effect of dating a number of events in 1 Maccabees a year later than in the chart above. In particular, it dates the desecration of the temple (1 Macc. 1.54) and dedication of the new altar (1 Macc. 4.52) to December 167 and December 164 respectively, which leaves no time for news of this to reach Antiochus before his death (see above). It would date Judas's siege of the citadel (if the date 150 in 1 Macc. 6.20 is a Jewish date) very late to summer 162 BCE; it would date the death of Nicanor (1 Macc. 7.43), and Bacchides's invasion and the death of Judas (1 Macc. 9.3) to 160 BCE; and similarly it would bring the date of the death of Alcimus (1 Macc. 9.54) down to 159 BCE. It would further bring down by one year various later dates: Jonathan's adoption of the high-priesthood (1 Macc. 10.21) would be dated 152 BCE; Simon's first year (1 Macc. 13.41) 142 BCE; the Jewish capture of the citadel 141 BCE; Simon's third year and the proclamation 140 BCE; and Simon's death to early 134 BCE. There is much to be said for datings from spring 312 BCE for the time of Judas, and much to be said for datings from the spring 311 BCE era for the time of Jonathan and Simon. The difficulty surfaces most evidently at the join between these two periods, at 1 Macc. 10.1, 21, when Alexander Balas appears and Jonathan accepts the high-priesthood. The root of the problem perhaps lies in the sources used by 1 Maccabees. The author of 1 Maccabees, however, seems to find no difficulty, even with 1 Macc. 10.1, 21, and he tells a coherent tale throughout, and offers a credible sequence of events. Major problems for the chronology of 1 Maccabees appear only if we confuse the issue by trying to integrate with the chronology of 1 Maccabees the information given by 2 Maccabees.

The Evidence of 2 Maccabees

At this point, therefore, we must examine briefly the basic problems raised for Maccabaean chronology by the presentation of events in 2 Maccabees. In many ways 1 Maccabees and 2 Maccabees are very different books. The author of 2 Maccabees is much more accessible to the reader, putting his personal signature clearly on his work in the prologue (2.19-30), the epilogue (15.37-39), and in several moralizing paragraphs inbetween (4.17; 5.17-20; 6.12-17; 12.43b-45). The author tells us in his prologue that he has written a one-volume abridgment of a five-volume work by Jason of Cyrene, who is otherwise completely unknown to us. The abridgment is often known as the Epitome, and its author as the Epitomist. His concern for Judaism is clear throughout; he uses the story of Judas to underline the importance of the temple, the law, the sabbath, prayer, loyalty under persecution, God's mercy to his covenant people, and the power of God's miraculous intervention on behalf of his people. He limits the scope of his history to the events preceding the rebellion and to the personal achievements of Judas in the reigns of Antiochus IV and Antiochus V (Eupator) (2.19-22), and says nothing of later events under Jonathan and Simon. To historians he is particularly interesting for his account of the political and religious background to the rebellion in chs. 4 and 5, and for various letters he preserves (1.1–2.18; 11.16-38).

The sequence of events in 1 Maccabees and 2 Maccabees is similar, but not identical. There are four particular disagreements between them which have given rise to much scholarly discussion. They concern (1) Antiochus's Egyptian campaigns and associated visits to Jerusalem in 169 and 168 BCE (1 Macc. 1.20-28; 2 Macc. 5.15-21); (2) the timing of the Maccabees' flight to the hills (1 Macc. 2.28) or wilderness (2 Macc. 5.27); (3) the date of Lysias's first campaign (1 Macc. 4.28-35; 2 Macc. 11.1-13); and (4) the relative sequence of the death of Antiochus IV and the dedication of the temple (1 Macc. 4.36-59; 6.1-17; 2 Macc. 9.1-29; 10.1-9).

(1) *Antiochus's Egyptian campaigns and subsequent events.* The first reference in Jewish literature to these events occurs in Dan. 11.28-31:

(28) He [Antiochus IV] shall return to his land [after negotiations with Ptolemy], with great wealth, but his heart shall be set against the holy covenant. He shall work his will, and return to his own land. (29) At the time

appointed he shall return and come into the south, but this time it shall not
be as it was before. (30) For the ships of Kittim [Romans] shall come against
him, and he shall lose heart and withdraw. He shall be enraged and take
action against the holy covenant. He shall turn back and pay heed to those
who forsake the holy covenant. (31) Forces sent by him shall occupy and
profane the temple and fortress. They shall abolish the regular burnt offering
and set up the abomination that makes desolate.

These verses suggest that in 169 BCE Antiochus 'worked his will'
against the Jews (exactly how is not stated) before returning to Syria,
and that the next year, in 168 BCE, after retreating from Egypt under
Roman pressure, he 'took action against the holy covenant', apparently
by sending forces to occupy and profane the temple and fortress.
1 Macc. 1.20-28 says that in 169 BCE Antiochus, after subduing Egypt,
entered and plundered the temple before returning to Syria. 1 Macc.
1.29-35 refers to the sending of an official in the following year, 168
BCE ('two years later' being understood as inclusive dating), who plun-
ders the city and fortifies a citadel (cf. 2 Macc. 5.24–26). 2 Macc. 5.15-
21 says that after his second invasion of Egypt (2 Macc. 5.1, 168 BCE)
Antiochus entered the temple (guided by Menelaus) and plundered it.
The content and relationship of these statements in Daniel 11, 1
Maccabees 1, and 2 Maccabees 5 have been much discussed. Certainly
1 Macc. 1.20-28 and 2 Macc. 5.15-21 both describe a temple plundering by Antiochus personally, but in different years. Daniel 11.30-31
might refer to the events of 168 BCE and suggest a temple plundering
(if 'profane the temple' can be interpreted that way) but, on the other
hand, Dan. 11.30-31 might refer rather to the desecration of the temple described in 1 Macc. 1.54, making no reference to any previous
plundering of the temple. Perhaps the most likely answer to this confusion is that 1 Macc. 1.20 correctly relates Antiochus's visit to Jerusalem
and his temple plundering to 169 BCE, and that 2 Macc. 5.15-21
wrongly attributes the plundering of the temple to the following year.
Each author accuses Antiochus personally of temple robbery, and each
author has Antiochus personally visit Jerusalem once—1 Maccabees,
after Antiochus's return from Egypt in 169 BCE (1 Maccabees does not
mention another campaign in Egypt), and 2 Maccabees after
Antiochus's second invasion of Egypt (2 Maccabees does not describe
the first campaign in Egypt). Each author therefore dates the temple
plundering to the only occasion open to him.

(2) 1 Macc. 2.28 says that Mattathias and his sons fled to the hills
after the king's officers began to enforce Antiochus's decree through
the cities of Judah; 2 Macc. 5.27 says that Judas and about nine others

got away to the wilderness and mountains, to avoid defilement, shortly before the decree (2 Macc. 6.1). Accuracy may lie with 1 Maccabees here; 2 Maccabees emphasizes Judas as leader rather than Mattathias, and has Judas out of Jerusalem before defilement appears there (2 Macc. 6.2).

(3) Lysias's first campaign is placed quite differently in the two books. 1 Macc. 4.28-35 places Judas's defeat of Lysias as the climax of a series of victories against Seleucid armies immediately before the cleansing of the sanctuary in Jerusalem (4.36-59). The parallel passage in 2 Macc. 11.1-13 is located after the cleansing of the sanctuary, in the reign of Antiochus V Eupator. (It has sometimes been argued that 1 Macc. 4.28-35 is a feebler doublet of 1 Macc. 6.28-47 [Lysias's second, and successful, campaign], but, as this has its parallel in 2 Macc. 13.1-3, 9-26, we would have to suppose that the doublet existed in the source of both 1 and 2 Maccabees, and so existed very early in the tradition.) The defeat of Lysias in 165 BCE, *before* the cleansing of the sanctuary and before the death of Antiochus IV, is supported by the dating and contents of correspondence from Lysias and Antiochus IV from 164 BCE, preserved in 2 Maccabees 11, which shows that Lysias and Antiochus IV were entering negotiations with the Jews (2 Macc. 11.13-15). 1 Maccabees, it is true, does not show Lysias offering negotiations until after his second campaign (6.55-59) after Antiochus IV's death, but the evidence of the correspondence of 2 Macc. 11.16-21, 27-33, 34-38 is decisive. (For full discussion of this correspondence, see pp. 49-52.)

(4) The most obvious difference in sequence of events between 1 and 2 Maccabees is that 1 Maccabees sets the restoration of the sanctuary before the death of Antiochus IV while 2 Maccabees reverses the order. We may compare the way in which 1 Maccabees places Lysias's first campaign before the death of Antiochus, while 2 Maccabees places it after. It may be that 2 Maccabees is following a different source, but it may also be that 2 Maccabees is rearranging material from his source for his own literary or theological reasons. An examination of the structure of 2 Maccabees shows that the narrative is formed in two parts, each with its own climax. The first climax is Judas's defeat of Nicanor, the death of Antiochus IV, and the celebration of the cleansing of the sanctuary (8.1–10.8). The second, parallel, climax is the defeat and death of Nicanor, and the decree establishing the future celebration of Nicanor's Day (15.6-36). The work (apart from the prefixed letters in 1.1–2.18) is structured as follows:

Prologue   2.19-32

Part I

(a)   3.1–6.17   Attacks on the Jewish temple and religion under
                     Seleucus IV and Antiochus IV: Antiochus's threat to
                     the temple and persecution of Jews
(b)   6.18–7.42   Martyrdom of Eleazar, the seven brothers and their
                     mother
(c)   8.1–10.9   Defeat of Nicanor; death of Antiochus; celebration of
                     temple purification

Part II

(d)   10.10–14.36   Attacks on the Jews under Antiochus V Eupator and
                     Demetrius: Nicanor's threat to the temple
(e)   14.37-46   Suicide of Razis
(f)   15.1-36   Defeat and death of Nicanor, and decree for future cel-
                     ebration of Nicanor's Day

Epilogue   15.37-39

We have similarly structured halves. In the first half, chs. 3–5 give us
much detail, mostly absent from 1 Maccabees, about political events
under Seleucus IV and Antiochus IV leading up to Antiochus's decree
(6.1-11); the decree is followed by the martyrdoms (6.18–7.42).
2 Maccabees then describes one major Seleucid invasion, led by
Nicanor, which Judas repels (8.1-36, apart from 8.30-33, which are an
intrusion here). This is in contrast to 1 Maccabees, which at this point
presents a series of Seleucid campaigns reaching a climax in Lysias's first
campaign. 2 Maccabees completes the first part with the death of
Antiochus and the purification of the sanctuary. In the second half, the
author has grouped under the reign of Antiochus V (10.14-38; 12.2-
38; cf. 8.30-33) a sequence of Seleucid attacks on the Jews by Gorgias,
Timothy and Lysias, almost all of which appears in 1 Maccabees 3–5 in
the period before the death of Antiochus. Under Demetrius's reign is
gathered material about Alcimus and Nicanor. In each half, the attacks
on the Jews are followed by the description of Jewish martyrdoms (Part
I) or a Jewish suicide (Part II), in turn followed by the death of the
enemy leader (Part I, Antiochus; Part II, Nicanor), and a Jewish celebration (Part I, purification of the sanctuary; Part II, Nicanor's Day). In
particular, Part I (c) and II (f) are carefully balanced and follow the
same sequence: defeat of Nicanor, death of Antiochus/Nicanor, and
celebration.

    Thus there are signs of the careful grouping and artificial arrange-
ment of material, giving a sequence of events quite different from that

in 1 Maccabees. It is important to note that, while 1 Maccabees orders events chronologically, with a fairly comprehensive list of dates taken from Seleucid and Jewish sources, 2 Maccabees gives no absolute dates apart from 13.1 (which dates the attack of Eupator and Lysias to year 149, probably autumn 163 BCE) and 14.4 which says that Alcimus went to king Demetrius 'in *about* the one hundred and fifty-first year', i.e. autumn 162–161 BCE, and those in the correspondence preserved in chs. 1–2, and ch. 11. Dates in 2 Maccabees are vaguely given: 'while the holy city was inhabited in unbroken peace' (3.1); 'When Seleucus died' (4.7); 'when the quadrennial games were being held at Tyre' (4.18); 'About this time Antiochus made his second invasion of Egypt' (5.1); 'Not long after this' (6.1); 'About that time...Antiochus had retreated' (9.1); 'after a lapse of two years' (10.3); 'Very soon after this' (11.1); 'Three years later' (14.1); 'about the one hundred and fifty-first year' (14.4). While the Epitomist of 2 Maccabees may have preserved from his source, Jason of Cyrene, much historical detail of genuine value, it is clearly difficult to use 2 Maccabees for the precise dating or sequence of events, and the sequence given by 1 Maccabees is generally to be preferred.

The Correspondence in 2 Macc. 11.16-38

We may now turn to the evidence of the letters in ch. 11. After an account of the defeat of Lysias and Lysias's proposal that matters be settled on just terms (11.1-15), 2 Maccabees inserts four letters that relate to negotiations between the Seleucids and the Jews (11.16-38). In 2 Maccabees these events take place after the death of Antiochus IV and the purification of the sanctuary, and apparently in the reign of Antiochus V (chs. 9 and 10). However, as we have seen, 2 Macc. 11.1-15 refers to Lysias's first campaign, which 1 Maccabees places (4.26-35) before the cleansing of the sanctuary (4.36-59) and the death of Antiochus (6.1-17). When we examine the letters in 2 Maccabees 11, it becomes clear that at least three of them also refer to this period after the defeat of Lysias and before the death of Antiochus IV. The dating of the letters is inconsistent with their present context in 2 Maccabees, and demonstrates that the sequence of events in 2 Maccabees is incorrect.

The first letter, 11.16-21, is from Lysias to the people of the Jews, and dated '148th year, Dioscorinthios 24th'. The year runs from autumn 165 BCE; the month name is otherwise unattested, and remains unexplained. Suggestions include Dios (the first month of the Seleucid autumnal calendar, i.e. October), Dioscouros (a Cretan autumnal month name), or Dystros (i.e. approximately February in the Seleucid calendar); but it is not clear how such well-known month names as Dios and Dystros might have become altered in this way. However, Lysias refers to proposals from Jewish (probably Maccabaean) representatives that he has put before the king (in year 148, Antiochus IV), who has accepted them; details may now be considered. The authenticity of this letter is generally accepted. It is usually dated between October 165 and February 164 BCE; Habicht, however, dates it with the Roman letter to summer or early autumn 164 BCE.

The second letter (11.22-26) is from king Antiochus to Lysias, and is undated. As the sender refers to his father's death, the sender is almost certainly Antiochus V, Eupator. The king instructs Lysias to inform the Jews that the temple may be restored to them (this is no major concession, for the Jews have already taken it) and they may live according to their ancestral laws. This announcement of the policy of the new regime would come appropriately at the beginning of Eupator's reign, and may belong therefore early in 163 BCE, soon after Antiochus IV's death and before Lysias's second campaign (the letter knows nothing of campaigns and negotiations). K.-D. Schunk and others have argued that this letter was a forgery, on the grounds that its attitude was too sympathetic to the Jews, that it was unlikely that the young king would be allowed to make such far-reaching decisions, and that this was an internal letter to which, if authentic, the Jewish writer could have no access; but the policy is appropriate enough to the occasion, and if Lysias was to proclaim it, there is no reason why the Jews should not have a copy of it.

The third letter (11.27-33) is from King Antiochus to the Senate of the Jews and to the other Jews, and is dated to the 148th year, Xanthicus 15th. If this date is to be taken at face value, this letter is dated 12 March 164 BCE, and the sender is Antiochus IV (though Goldstein argues for Antiochus V as co-regent in Antiochus IV's absence in Persia). The king himself writes formally to the Senate (*gerousia*) of the Jews and to the other Jews—presumably to the official council and to the Maccabaean party—to advise them of an amnesty until the end of the month Xanthicus (the end of the year on the Babylonian and Jewish spring dating for the new year). Those who accept it will be allowed to enjoy their own food (*dapan mata*; perhaps read *diaitēmata*, 'customs'; Goldstein, *II Macc.*, p. 421) and other laws.

3. *Chronology and Sequence*	51

The king has been informed by the high-priest Menelaus, whom he is sending back to the Jews 'to encourage' them. This reference to Menelaus (the king's protégé, but unpopular in Jerusalem) underlines the authenticity of the document. The date, however, has raised questions; if the letter did not leave Antioch until Xanthicus 15th, would it reach Jerusalem in time for an amnesty due to expire on the 30th Xanthicus to be meaningful? Habicht thinks not; the letter would have been sent earlier, probably in autumn 165 BCE, the date (11.33) being wrongly applied from the following letter (11.34-38). Goldstein relates the arrival of the letter to the statement in *Megillat Ta'anit* that on 28 Adar (= Xanthicus) 'the good news came to the Jews, that they did not have to depart from the Torah'. Goldstein notes that a message sent from Antioch on the 15th Xanthicus could easily reach Jerusalem by the 28th, and, as Judas was a compact area, news of the offer to end the persecution could spread quickly; 'thus the dates in our letter are by no means incredible' (*II Macc.*, pp. 418-19).

The final letter in the collection (11.34-38), from Quintus Memmius and Titus Manius, envoys of the Romans, to the people of the Jews, is clearly closely related to the first letter (cf. v. 35), and presumably dates from a little later in Seleucid year 148 (i.e. autumn 165–164 BCE). It is the earliest evidence of Roman contact with the Jews. Whichever Jewish party invited Roman support, the Romans were probably pleased enough to have an excuse to put pressure on the Seleucid king. The authenticity of this letter is undoubted, but the names of the envoys and the date of the letter are both questionable. The original letter presumably had a Roman, not a Seleucid, date, the Seleucid date being acquired from a Jerusalem archivist, or perhaps deriving from 11.33 when the two letters were brought into association. In some Latin texts the month name has been taken from the first letter, v. 21, the scribe obviously noting the connection of the two letters. Of the envoys, Quintus Memmius is otherwise totally unknown (though this is no reason for rejecting his involvement); the name Titus Manius is suspect, because Manius is more likely as the *praenomen* (forename) than the *nomen gentilicium* (family name), and the third name, the *cognomen*, is not given. The historian Polybius names a Manius Sergius as a Roman ambassador (with Gaius Sulpicius) to Antiochus IV and Eumenes II of Pergamum in the mid-160s BCE, and Codex Venetus gives the name of our ambassador as T. Manius Ernius. Putting these pieces of evidence together, B. Niese proposed Manius Sergius as the original name of the ambassador mentioned in 2 Macc. 11.34, but Ernius is not a natural

error for Sergius, perhaps rather reflecting some name with the ending
-anius or -ianus, and we would still have to account for the introduction of the *praenomen* Titus. The name remains uncertain, and the person unidentified.

The net result of this exploration of 2 Maccabees is that, at least in
the form left to us by the Epitomist of 2 Maccabees, the chronology
and sequence of events in 2 Maccabees cannot be trusted. It is the
result of Jason's scheme in five books (2.23), its modification by the
Epitomist, and the latter's intention 'to please those who wish to read,
to make it easy for those who are inclined to memorize', 'leaving the
responsibility for exact details to the compiler, while devoting our
effort to arriving at the outlines of the condensation' (Prologue, 2.25,
28).

Further Reading

There is an enormous amount of scholarly literature on this subject. Much detailed
analysis will be found in the commentaries, especially those by F.-M. Abel and J.A.
Goldstein (who gives a table of his reconstruction of the sequence of events).

On Maccabaean Chronology:

E.J. Bickerman, *Chronology of the Ancient World* (rev. edn; London: Thames & Hudson,
    1980). A useful general introduction to the problem of dating events in the ancient
    world.
K. Bringmann, *Hellenistische Reform und Religionsverfolgung in Judäa* (AAWG,
    Philologische-historische Klasse, 3. 132; Göttingen: Vandenhoeck & Ruprecht,
    1983). The first chapter contains an important discussion on the dates of 1
    Maccabees.
J. Bunge, 'Zur Geschichte und Chronologie des Untergangs der Oniaden und des
    Aufstiegs der Hasmonäer', *JSJ* 6 (1976), pp. 1-46.
T. Fischer, *Seleukiden und Makkabäer* (Bochum: Studienverlag Brockmeyer, 1980).
R. Hanhart, 'Zur Zeitrechnung des I und II Makkabäerbuches', in A. Jepsen and
    R.Hanhard (eds.), *Untersuchungen zur israelitische-jüdischen Chronologie* (BZAW, 88;
    Berlin: W. de Gruyter 1964). pp. 49-96
K.-D. Schunk, *Die Quellen des I und II Makkabäerbuches* (Halle: Niemeyer, 1954).

On the Date of the Death of Antiochus IV and the Rededication of the Temple

M.J. Dagut, '2 Maccabees and the Death of Antiochus IV Epiphanes', *JBL* 72 (1953), pp.
    149-57.
L.L. Grabbe, 'Maccabean Chronology: 167–164 or 168–165 BCE', *JBL* 110 (1991), pp.
    59-74.
A.J. Sachs and D.J. Wiseman, 'A Babylonian Kinglist of the Hellenistic Period', *Iraq* 16
    (1954), pp. 202-12.

3. *Chronology and Sequence* 53

J. Schaumberger, 'Die neue Seleukidenliste BM 35603 und die makkabäische Chronologie', *Biblica* 36 (1955), pp. 423-35.

J.C. VanderKam, 'Hanukkah: Its Timing and Significance According to 1 and 2 Maccabees', *JSP* 1 (1987), pp. 23-40.

On the Correspondence of 2 Maccabees 11

C. Habicht, 'Royal Documents in Maccabees II', *HSCP* 80 (1976), pp. 1-18.

C. Habicht, *II Makkabäerbuch* (JSHRZ 1.3; Gütersloh: Gerd Mohn, 1976).

J. Goldstein, *II Maccabees* (Anchor Bible 41A; Garden City, NY: Doubleday, 1983).

4

CHAPTERS 1 AND 2:
THE DECREE OF ANTIOCHUS

In the first three chapters of this study we have examined the origins of
1 Maccabees, the composition and structure of the book, and the complexities of its chronology. These are necessary preliminaries for any
scholarly attempt to understand the course of Maccabaean history, to
which we now turn. In the next three chapters we shall examine the
history of the Maccabaean struggle as it is presented in 1 Maccabees.
These next three chapters are not a running commentary on 1 Maccabees, but an attempt to examine and assess the historical picture it presents of the Maccabaean rebellion. We shall inevitably refer to 2
Maccabees where necessary, but our primary concern is with 1
Maccabees, and detailed examination of 2 Maccabees and its very different presentation of events must be left to another volume of this
series (for a preliminary sketch of 2 Maccabees, see above, pp. 45-49).
We begin with a fairly full examination of 1 Maccabees 1–2, where we
are immediately confronted by two major issues: the background to the
rebellion, and the reason for Antiochus's decree and the ensuing religious persecution.

The Hellenistic Era

As we saw when examining the structure of 1 Maccabees, 1 Macc.
1.1–2.64 is in literary terms an introduction, setting the scene for the
work of Judas, and his brothers Jonathan and Simon. 1 Macc. 1.1-10
opens the story with a brief overview of the Hellenistic world from
Alexander the Great (356–323 BCE) to the accession in 175 BCE of the
Seleucid king Antiochus IV Epiphanes, son of Antiochus III. The
writer is well informed about Alexander's achievements, about his successors and the dynasties that followed them (he is certainly thinking

chiefly of the Ptolemies in Egypt and the Seleucids in Babylon and Syria), and admirably concise; but he allows himself three critical remarks which reveal his views. The first, 'He was exalted, and his heart was lifted up' (v. 3), criticizes Alexander for seeing himself in near divine terms (cf. Isa. 14.12-14, of the king of Assyria, or Ezek. 28.2-10, of the prince of Tyre). The second comments that the political descendants of Alexander 'caused many evils on the earth' (v. 9), and the third that Antiochus Epiphanes was 'a sinful root' (v. 10; cf. for the expression Isa. 11.1; Ecclus 47.22), that is, an offshoot, of the Seleucid dynasty. Antiochus gets a bad press in all the sources (cf. Dan. 7.11, 20; 8.9-12; 2 Macc. 9.1-28), and it is clear that Jewish tradition held him largely responsible for what happened.

The Beginning of the Trouble

Antiochus was not solely responsible, as the author of 1 Maccabees makes clear (1.11-15). Certain renegades from the Israelite community misled many, inviting them 'to make a covenant' with the surrounding Gentiles, blaming recent disasters on Jewish separatism. What separation and what consequential disasters were they thinking of, what did 'making a covenant' mean in this connection, and who were these renegades? The Jews saw themselves as separate from the Gentiles, and lobbied hard to be allowed to follow their ancestral laws; Antiochus III, on taking over Palestine in 200 BCE, had allowed the Jewish nation a form of government in accordance with their ancestral laws and had offered them favourable concessions, giving explicit support to their law excluding foreigners from the temple (Josephus, *Ant.* 12.138-46). Greek writers such as Hecataeus of Abdera (c. 300 BCE) recognized the distinct nature of the Jewish polity. The renegades are aware both of the conservative Jewish attitude to the Gentiles and of the corresponding Gentile attitude towards the Jews, and apparently believe that in the modern Hellenistic world the Jewish nation is not helped by distancing itself. (Similarly, there are those in our own day in Europe who believe strongly that their country, with its distinctive way of life or government, should remain separate from European union, and those who equally strongly believe that they should embrace it.) The Seleucid Empire had been relatively kind to the Jews until Seleucus IV's attempt to raid the Jerusalem temple treasury, but this attempt had failed and disaster had been averted. By 'disasters' the renegades may have meant little more than what they perceived as the disadvantages of not belonging to the eastern Mediterranean Hellenistic club.

What the renegades wanted is clear from what, with the king's permission, they proceeded to do. They built a gymnasium (1 Macc. 1.14; according to 2 Macc. 4.9, a gymnasium and an *ephebeion*) in Jerusalem. The *epheboi* were originally the young men in training for war;

> by hellenistic times the *ephebeia* had become an exclusive municipal male finishing school housed in the gymnasium where future aristocrats (*epheboi*) leisurely pursued their studies with an emphasis on physical education...Study in the *ephebeia* certified that one was truly civilized (i.e., Hellenized) and was essential for full social and political acceptance' (Townsend, ABD II.315).

The renegades were thus setting up one of the essential prerequisites of any Hellenistic city; a fully developed city would include also one or more temples, a citadel (cf. 2 Macc. 4.12), a council house, a treasury (cf. 1 Macc. 14.49), a public theatre for assemblies of various kinds, a gymnasium, a wrestling arena (*palaistra*, 2 Macc. 4.14), a stadium, and perhaps a hippodrome. These 'renegades' were essentially members of the richer classes of Jerusalem with some knowledge of how things were done abroad, and anxious, perhaps partly for reasons of national pride and partly for personal economic reasons, to 'join with the Gentiles', that is, with the Hellenistic common market.

Fuller details of this important social and political change are given in 2 Macc. 4.7-17, where it is made clear that it involved not only 'the noblest of the young men' (2 Macc. 4.12) but also the priests (2 Macc. 4.14), and that the change was effected by the high-priest, Jason, as part of a major political endeavour 'to enrol the people of Jerusalem as citizens of Antioch' (2 Macc. 4.9). The precise translation and meaning of this phrase (*tous en hierosolumois Antiocheis anagrapsai*) has been hotly debated. There are two main proposals, the first associated with E.J. Bickerman (*The God of the Maccabees*, trans. H.R. Moehring, 1979, pp. 39-41), and the second with V. Tcherikover (*Hellenistic Civilization and the Jews*, trans. S. Applebaum, 1966, pp. 161-69). The first translates the Greek phrase as 'to register the Jerusalem Antiochenes', that is to make a list of the privileged few who would be known as Jerusalem Antiochenes (cf. 2 Macc. 4.19, 'Antiochian citizens from Jerusalem') These people would form a separate community or corporation within the wider population, and such groups were known in the Hellenistic Near East as *politeumata*. The second proposal involves a different translation of the phrase, 'to register the people of Jerusalem as Antiochenes'. This implies that the change sought and obtained by the renegades was to turn the men of Jerusalem into citizens of a Greek

polis, perhaps to be called Antioch-at-Jerusalem, with all that might
imply for status and privileges within the empire. Tcherikover rightly
notes that in Greek cities there was a difference between citizens and
mere inhabitants, and that not all the inhabitants of Jerusalem became
Antiochenes automatically. Citizenship would be restricted to the ruling aristocracy. 'What the "Antiochenes" sought was sociopolitical
privilege and status, better cosmopolitan communications, above all
with the Seleucid court' (P. Green, *Alexander to Actium*, 1990, p. 510).

Thus on either translation and interpretation, the renegades' proposals meant a new Hellenistic constitution, with power limited (as before)
to the aristocracy, in which the priests were well represented. It did not
mean any change in religious belief or practice, or any alteration in the
status of the Jewish law, the Torah. The author of 1 Maccabees, however, disapproves of this association with the Gentiles (1.15), but says
nothing at all about the situation in Jerusalem between the introduction
of the gymnasium and the Egyptian campaigns of Antiochus IV. It is
left to 2 Maccabees to name the high-priest, Jason, and to describe his
replacement by Menelaus, whose scandalous theft of sacred vessels from
the temple caused riots, deaths and corruption (2 Macc. 4.23-50). Why
1 Maccabees says so little of these events is not clear; he may be playing
them down to focus more on Antiochus and the achievement of the
Maccabaean family.

The Events of 170–168 BCE

Antiochus IV's father, Antiochus III, had won Coele-Syria and
Phoenicia (including Palestine) from Egypt at the battle of Paneion in
200 BCE, and Egypt nursed the desire to regain her lost province. Egypt
claimed that Antiochus III had promised Coele-Syria as a dowry for his
daughter Cleopatra when she married Ptolemy V Epiphanes in 193
BCE. When Antiochus IV took the Seleucid throne in 175 BCE,
Ptolemy Philometor VI (who was Antiochus's nephew) was a minor,
under the control of two court officials, Eulaeus and Lenaeus. About
173 BCE, Antiochus sent Apollonios son of Menestheus to Egypt for
the coming of age (in effect, the enthronement) of Philometor, learned
of Egypt's growing hostility and, in the interests of security, visited
Joppa and Jerusalem on his southern border, where he was welcomed
(2 Macc. 4.21-22). The Sixth Syrian War broke out in 170 BCE, Egypt
perhaps judging the Seleucid Empire to be unstable (Antiochus having
just murdered his co-regent, the young son of Seleucus IV), and Rome

to be no threat (being deeply involved in war in Macedonia). Both
sides sent missions to Rome late in 170 BCE, but meanwhile Antiochus
defeated the Egyptians at Mons Casius near Pelusium in November
170 BCE (1 Macc. 1.17-19). The winter was taken up by diplomatic
activity, which ended with Philometor in effect under Antiochus's
direction, and Antiochus left Egypt in summer 169 BCE. These events
are also recorded, somewhat cryptically, in Dan. 11.25-28.

1 Maccabees now relates that Antiochus visited Jerusalem with a
strong force and pillaged the temple, sacrilegiously entering the temple.
1 Maccabees gives no explanation, but the explanation is probably the
obvious one: that, after his Egyptian campaign, Antiochus needed
money, and looting temples was the well-tried way to raise it. It has
been argued by J. Goldstein, however, that the real purpose of
Antiochus's visit 'with a strong force' was not to raid the temple but to
suppress an attempt by Jason, the former high-priest of Jerusalem, to
remove Menelaus, who had supplanted him (2 Macc. 5.5-6).
2 Maccabees, however, locates Jason's assault on the city after
Antiochus's second return from Egypt, in 168 BCE, and there seems no
reason to doubt this dating (cf. E.S. Gruen, in P. Green, *Hellenistic
History and Culture*, 1993, p. 246 n. 22), for it explains the viciousness
of the reprisals on Jerusalem described in 1 Maccabees 129–35; 2 Macc.
5.11-14. The temple plundering of 2 Macc. 5.15-16 really belongs
where 1 Maccabees places it, in 169 BCE. (For the relationship of
1 Macc. 1.20-28 to the similar account in 2 Macc. 5.15-21, see above,
pp. 45-46.)

Certainly the looting of the temple would have caused considerable
anger in Jerusalem and Judaea, and will hardly have increased local support for the ruling clique, led by the high-priest. It is strange that again
1 Maccabees says nothing at this point, either of Antiochus IV's second
campaign in Egypt, resulting in his notorious expulsion in 168 BCE by
the Romans, or of political events in Jerusalem, where, according to
2 Macc. 5.5-10, the ejected Jason had tried to reinstate himself by
physical force. 1 Maccabees simply continues his narrative with
Jerusalem's next experience of Antiochus. 'Two years later' (which
may mean little more than a year after Antiochus's plundering of the
temple, and so in 168 BCE; cf. Grabbe, 1991, p. 68) the king sent a
chief collector of tribute to Jerusalem, with a large army; he plundered,
burned and destroyed the city, killed many of the men and took the
women and children and cattle, presumably to sell as slaves and booty.
Again, financial motives appear; but behind the Greek *archonta phorolo-*

gias, 'chief collector of tribute', may lie a mistranslation of the Hebrew for 'captain of the Mysians', that is a captain of mercenary troops named Apollonios in the similar story of 2 Macc. 5.24-26 which speaks of the capture of Jerusalem, with thousands killed and as many sold into slavery. (Two massacres within the year seems unlikely and these two stories look remarkably like two versions of the same event.)

1 Macc. 1.33 follows the massacre with the establishment of a well-defended citadel, which became a thorn in Jerusalem's side for the next 26 years. 2 Macc. 5.1, 11 sets the massacre after Antiochus's second return from Egypt, in 168 BCE, which agrees with the dating of 1 Macc. 1.29. These drastic events demand explanation, for until now Antiochus had no fault to find with Jerusalem, where, after all, his own protégé was high-priest, and had been instrumental in providing him with urgently needed money. What had happened to make Antiochus so vindictive, and why was a new citadel required to control Jerusalem? The standard explanation is that Antiochus, hearing of Jason's attack, interpreted it as a pro-Egyptian insurrection, and responded sharply. The citadel was obviously needed for military control of a city that could not be relied upon. Tcherikover has proposed that it was not Jason's attempted coup that brought Apollonios on the scene (for the coup failed), but a popular revolt against Jason, the hellenizing aristocracy, and their Seleucid supporters. 'It was not the revolt which came as a response to the persecution', Tcherikover argued, 'but the persecution which came as a response to the revolt' (p. 191). However, an attack on Menelaus would be seen by Antiochus as an attack on Seleucid rule, and his natural irritation, it is argued, would be sharpened to feelings of vengeance by his humiliation at the hands of the Roman envoy Popilius Laenas in Egypt.

The Location of the Akra

The location of the Seleucid citadel (the 'Akra') in Jerusalem remains one of the most vexed of topographical questions. The evidence for it is found principally in the *Letter of Aristeas* (a mid-second BCE document), 1 Maccabees (2 Maccabees does not refer to the Maccabaean period Akra), and from Josephus. All these authors probably had first-hand knowledge of Jerusalem, though only the author of the *Letter of Aristeas*, and the Jason of Cyrene whose work the author of 2 Maccabees abbreviated, could have known first-hand the Jerusalem of Maccabaean times. The *Letter of Aristeas* (chs. 100–104) says that the citadel (*akra*) was the special protection of the temple, to prevent entrance within the walls surrounding the temple. It was on a very high point, towering above the temple walls and fortified with towers on which were various war machines. This has points in common with Josephus's description of the *akra*, but it is not certain that it refers to the building that existed from 169–142 BCE; the author may be referring to an earlier or later citadel. 1 Macc. 1.33 describes the original building of the *akra*: 'they fortified the City of David with a great strong wall and strong towers, and it became their citadel'. It is apparently near enough to the sanctuary to control it (4.41; 6.18); it could be isolated from the city by a high wall (12.36); it was 'alongside' (or perhaps 'opposite'; Greek *para*) the temple hill (13.52); it was 'in the City of David' and from it attacks could be made to the environs of the sanctuary (14.36). It was 'in Jerusalem' (15.28).

Clearly the author of 1 Maccabees locates the citadel near the temple, and temple precincts are not safe from attack until the *akra* has been isolated. Scholars have located the *akra* at various points around the temple: at the north-west corner of the temple platform, the site of the Baris and the later Roman fort Antonia (recently, Goldstein, *I Macc.*, p. 214, and map 1, p. 528); on the western hill, in the upper City, overlooking the temple from across the Tyropoeon valley (Abel, Vincent, Avi-Yonah); at the Herodian citadel site by the Jaffa Gate (Kenyon); within the present Haram area, immediately north of the Double and Triple Gates, but south of the Hellenistic, pre-Herodian temple area (Wightman); at the south-east area of the Herodian temenos, immediately north of the 'straight joint' on the eastern wall of the temple platform (archaeological evidence is adduced in Hellenistic masonry foundations in the east wall north of the 'straight joint') (Tsafrir); on the south-east hill in the region of the Ophel (Shotwell). Thus the Akra has been located at almost every possible point in a ring round the temple area.

The problem has been complicated by the evidence of Josephus. Josephus knew his Jerusalem, but he too was interpreting the evidence of 1 Maccabees. Josephus divides Jerusalem into two major hills, the Upper City on the hill to the west of the Tyropoeon valley and the Lower City on the hill to the east (*War* 5.136-141). He is quite clear that the Akra belongs on the lower, that is eastern, hill (*War* 1.39; 5.137; 5.252, cf. 354; *Ant.* 12.252). Below the Akra, also on the east side of the Tyropoeon, was a third hill, once divided from the Akra by a broad ravine which the Hasmonaeans had filled up to unite the city to the temple (*War* 5.138). The Hasmonaeans 'also reduced the eleva-tion of the Akra by levelling its summit, in order that it might not block the view of the temple' (*War* 5.139, Loeb. trans.). (This third hill seems to be what was in earlier Israelite times known as the City of David.) In *War* 5.252 and 354, Josephus connects the Akra with the area of the palace of Helen, Queen of Adiabene. All this suggests that Josephus located the Akra on the south side of the temple, north of a ravine originally separating off the earlier City of David.

However, this picture is complicated by the fact that Josephus expressly says that the Akra was high enough to overlook the temple (*Ant.* 12.252), that it commanded the temple (*Ant.* 12.362), and that when Simon captured the Akra he razed it to the ground and levelled the hill on which it stood so that the temple might be higher than this (*War* 1.50; 5.138; 13.215-17). There are two major difficulties here: first, any such hill south of the temple mount area from which the Akra could dominate the temple, given the present southward slope of the land, must have been massive, and such major landscaping is most unlikely, even in the three years that Josephus allows. And secondly, though Josephus says that Simon razed the site of the Akra, 1 Maccabees says only that Simon expelled the garrison from the citadel (1 Macc. 13.50), strengthened the fortifications of the temple alongside (or over against) the citadel (13.52), and settled Jews in it and fortified it (14.37). 1 Maccabees does not say that it was razed, but that Simon took it over and fortified it for the safety of the country (14.37). It is tempting to believe, with Shotwell (*BASOR* 176, [1964], pp. 10-19) that Josephus got the location right but was wrong about the height. However, Josephus may be right, or almost right, on both counts if we accept the solution that the Akra lay immediately to the south, or south-east, of the Hellenistic temple area, but within the bounds of the later Herodian temenos, the present Haram. This makes good topographic sense. The Akra might then easily overlook the actual sanctuary, and the need to reduce its height becomes meaning-ful. A wall could easily then separate it from the Lower City (1 Macc. 12.36), and it could be accurately described as being 'alongside' the temple area (1 Macc. 13.52). The reduction of the level of the Akra, however, was the work, not of Simon, but of the later Hasmonaeans, as Josephus expressly says in *War* 5.139; his later attribution of this work to Simon in *Ant.*13.215-17 is then mistaken.

The Decree of Antiochus IV

The massacre, plundering and fortification of Jerusalem are followed in
1 Maccabees by the 'decree' (1.60) of Antiochus prohibiting the practice of Jewish religion. The instruction from Antiochus that 'all should
be one people, and that all should give up their particular customs' is
the author's fancy, perhaps deriving from stories such as Daniel 3, or
perhaps the author's misconstruction of an earlier invitation to a uni-
versally Hellenistic way of life (Goldstein, *I Macc.*, p. 120), but there is
no evidence that Antiochus ever intended religious coercion throughout his empire. The decree applied only to Jews in Jerusalem and
Judaea; Josephus tells us that the people of Samaria applied for, and got,
exemption (*Ant.* 12.260-61). The contents of the decree are given in
1.44-50, from which it appears that the daily temple offering (the
tamid, i.e. burnt offering, sacrifices and drink offering; cf. Num. 28.3-8)
and circumcision were forbidden, sabbaths and feasts were to be pro-
faned, the sanctuary and its holy things (not 'priests' as in NRSV) were
to be defiled; positively, altars and sacred precincts and shrines were to
be built for idols, and swine and unclean animals were to be sacrificed.
Disobedience was to be punished by death. This decree, prohibiting
sabbath, circumcision, temple and legal offerings alike, hit directly at
the core of Judaism; the command to build shrines and make offerings
to idols forced Jews to break the fundamental commandment prohibiting idolatry (Exod. 20.4-6; Deut. 5.8-10), and the Deuteronomic law
of one place of worship (Deut. 12). (2 Macc. 6 goes much further; the
Jerusalem temple was to be renamed the temple of Olympian Zeus,
and was defiled by debauched behaviour and forbidden offerings, and
Jews were made to share in Gentile sacrifices on the monthly celebration of the king's birthday, and take part in processions in honour of
the Greek god Dionysus.)

The purpose of such an unusual decree has been much debated. E.S.
Gruen (in P. Green, *Hellenistic History and Culture*, 1993, pp. 250-64)
considers the main explanations offered.

(1) 'Antiochus saw himself as a crusader for Hellenism, and
attempted to impose conformity on his realm' (p. 250). But while
Antiochus projected himself as a great benefactor to the Greeks, there
is little evidence for this thesis in the eastern parts of the empire. He
did not see himself as the incarnation of Zeus Olympios or seek to
impose that cult upon his kingdom. 'Ideological fervour did not char-
acterize the schemes of Antiochus IV' (p. 252).

(2) 'The motives that drove Antiochus were practical and political: cash for his military adventures and security for his position in Palestine' (p. 253). Thus Antiochus had to shore up Menelaus's regime, even when it came to supporting Menelaus in religious persecution. Antiochus needed money, especially in 169 BCE for his Egyptian campaigns. But the Seleucid Empire was far from insolvent, and Menelaus was not to be kept in power (assuming that was necessary) by religious persecution. Menelaus as high-priest would hardly 'foster a policy calculated to spark explosive upheaval' (p. 254).

(3) Antiochus, a former hostage in Rome, drew his inspiration from Roman colonial practice. The establishment of the Antiochenes in Jerusalem copied the Roman practice of extending Roman citizenship to Italian communities, and the outlawing of Jewish religion copied Roman measures against the cult of Bacchus (Dionysus) in Rome. But it is unlikely that a hostage developed such knowledge of Roman colonial practice; the initiative for the Antiochenes in Jerusalem came from Jason and the 'renegades'; and 'the Romans professed to be cracking down on an alien creed, foreign to national traditions, whereas Antiochus imposed an alien creed while seeking to eradicate a national tradition' (p. 255). (According to 2 Macc. 6.7, Antiochus seems to have imposed Bacchic/Dionysiac cultic practices!)

(4) Antiochus was an eccentric. But this is belied by his political, diplomatic and miltary successes.

(5) The blame really lay with Jewish Hellenizers, and the resultant struggle between Hellenizers and traditionalists, between Judaism and Hellenism, leading to the persecution of the religious conservatives. But confrontation between Judaism and Hellenism is not a central or repeated theme of contemporary literature (e.g. the Wisdom of Ben Sira or the book of Daniel) nor even of 1 Maccabees. Jason's innovations in 2 Maccabees are not unlawful, and his representatives at the games at Tyre did not compromise their Jewish beliefs. Menelaus is not accused of Hellenism, or persuading the king to persecute his co-religionists (indeed, he helped arrange an amnesty for the rebels, 2 Macc. 11.29), but of stealing temple vessels to raise money for the king, of bribery, and of arranging murder.

(6) Antiochus intended to compensate for his loss of face at Eleusis in Egypt and to overawe his empire by demonstrating his control over his Jewish subjects. This was followed up by his display of power at the parade of his armed forces at Daphne near Antioch in 166 BCE. This is Gruen's proposal (Gruen, 'Hellenism and Persecution', 1993, pp. 260-

64). The obvious objection to this thesis is that destruction of the Jews
is not much to throw into the scales against defeat by the power of
Rome—though perhaps something was better than nothing.

(7) P. Green (*Alexander to Actium*, 1990, p. 516) offers another suggestion: the edict of religious persecution 'was directly aimed at
Jerusalem and Judaea, where it was hand-delivered in written form'.
'All he [Antiochus] aimed to achieve was the elimination of a rebellious
local group by abolishing the ideological code that sustained it' (Green,
p. 516). Antiochus's motive was purely pragmatic and political. This is
the simplest solution, and perhaps makes the best sense.

'The Abomination of Desolation'

The decree itself was followed by a series of deliberately provocative
acts: the desecration of the altar of burnt offering outside the temple;
the building of altars throughout the cities of Judah; the destruction of
books of the law; and finally, as a climax, the offering of illegal sacrifice
'on the altar which was upon the altar of burnt offering' (1 Macc. 1.54-
59). The dates of the desecration of the altar, and the sacrifice upon it,
were remembered—the 15th and 25th days of Kislev, in the 145th year
(168 BCE)—and clearly these events were seen as the ultimate sacrilege.
It is less clear exactly what they involved.

1 Macc. 1.54 speaks of the erection of 'a desolating sacrilege (Greek,
bdēlugma erēmōseōs, 'abomination of desolation') upon the altar of burnt
offering'; compare Dan. 11.31, 'abomination that makes desolate'
(Hebrew *haš-šiqqūṣ mešômēm*), and variants of this phrase in Dan. 8.13;
9.27; 12.11. (This powerful phrase is remembered and reused in the
New Testament; cf. Mk 13.14; Mt. 24.15.) The first question is, what
does this phrase mean? The usual explanation is that it is a derogatory
parody on the Syrian god called in Aramaic Ba 'al Samen, 'Lord of
Heaven'; *šiqqūṣ* ('something appalling', 'abomination') standing for the
foreign god Ba 'al (just as *bôsheth*, 'shame', can replace Ba 'al in some
Hebrew names, e.g. Mephibosheth, 2 Sam. 4.4), and *šômēm* ('desolating') punning on *šamēm* (heaven). This 'god of heaven' is then related
to the Zeus Olympios ('Olympian Zeus') of 2 Macc. 6.1, in whose
honour the Jerusalem temple was rededicated. In this case, Antiochus
has perhaps proposed that the Jews worship an alternative deity, or
rather, the image or statue of such a deity, for the reference appears to
be to a physical artefact that has been erected. But there is no suggestion that a cult image is intended until later Christian writers. Bar

Kochva (*Judas Maccabaeus*, p. 248) also takes šāmēm as 'desolating', but in the literal, active sense; the abomination makes the temple desolate, or empty, of pilgrims and their sacrifices. What then was the abomination? In the Hebrew scriptures, 'abomination' is a term associated with idolatry (cf. Deut. 7.25-26; 2 Kgs 21.2-5, where Manasseh follows the abominable practices (Hebrew, *tô 'ābôt*; Greek, *bdēlugmata*) of other nations, erecting altars for Ba ʿal and all the host of heaven). The word šām m may also be construed as meaning not 'desolating' but 'appalling'. The phrase may then be translated 'an appalling sacrilege' (though in view of the word 'erected', something solid must be in mind). Antiochus has therefore erected something idolatrous, though not an actual image. What was this object? 1 Macc. 1. 59 speaks of 'the altar (Greek, *bōmos,* i.e. a pagan altar) that was on top of the altar of burnt offering', and 4.43 refers to the removal of 'defiled stones', or 'stones of abomination' from the sanctuary, which may be the stones of the altar of 1 Macc. 1.59. The sacrilegious artefact was probably some form of pagan altar, mounted on the temple's original altar of burnt offering.

Goldstein argues that the implication of šāmēm (punning on the word for 'heaven') is that Antiochus used meteorites (i.e. stones from heaven) as idolatrous objects of worship (*I Macc.*, p. 147), following the ancient Near Eastern tradition of setting up cult-stones as representative of a deity (*maṣṣebôt,* cf. Exod. 23.24, or, in Greek, *baituloi* or *baitylia)*, and so enforcing upon the Jews a religion like that of their Syrian and Phoenician neighbours (*ibid.*, p.157). There are several problems with Goldstein's view: (1) the 'defiled stones' of 4.43 are not said to have been upon the altar; (2) there is no indication that Antiochus placed *three* objects on the altar of burnt offering; (3) the idea that the desolating sacrilege on the altar was a meteorite from heaven seems far-fetched—a meteorite would not in itself be a sacrilegious object; and (4) the idea that these stones (the text of 1.59 speaks only of an altar) were linked with the three gods Zeus, Athene and Dionysus is purely speculative.

Mattathias and the Hasidaeans

From the Jewish point of view, temple plundering and massacre could be borne, but the prohibition of fundamental Jewish religious practices and the imposition of something that could be seen as idolatrous could not, and it was clearly the view of 1 Maccabees that the persecution led to the rebellion (1 Macc. 2). The structure and concerns of ch. 2 have already been considered (p. 24-25); here we are concerned with ch. 2 as evidence for the beginnings of the Maccabaean movement. Mattathias (v. 1), unmentioned in 2 Maccabees, is identified as of priestly family. Five sons are listed in v. 2, each with a nickname; the author probably draws this list from an independent source, for it does not correspond with the picture given elsewhere in 1 Maccabees, which (Judas and Eleazar apart) gives no nicknames and presents the brothers in a different sequence. The story of Mattathias's reaction to the invitation to offer sacrifice on the unlawful altar in Modein (vv. 15-26) presents Mattathias as a shining example of religious correctitude, rejecting apostasy in the manner of a Phinehas (Num. 25) by slaying both the offender and the person who invited the offence. This story has all the marks of the story-teller, and is hardly from an official chronicle. Verses 29-38 tell of one loyal group who tried to evade the decree by disappearing into the wilderness (thus also evading taxation); when attacked on the sabbath they refused to sacrifice their principles by defending themselves, and were killed. This is developed into a justification of the Maccabaean readiness to fight on the sabbath if necessary (vv. 39-41). The pacific response of this group is then contrasted with the military response of the Hasidim, who organized an army and struck down sinners, and of the friends of Mattathias, who forcibly circumcised all the uncircumcised boys they found, and so rescued the law out of the hand of the Gentiles and kings (42-48). All this material is *haggadah*, designed to illustrate by example the correct responses to the royal decree. The stories are vaguely set in the period after the decree and before Mattathias's death in year 146 (167–166 BCE), and they give little hard information.

The identity and the role of the Hasidaeans (1 Macc. 2.42; 7.14; 2 Macc. 14.6) have been much discussed. Their name derives from the Hebrew word *ḥasîdîm* familiar in the Psalms (e.g. 79.2; 149.1), where it refers generally to pious Israelites faithful to God, but the early translator of 1 Maccabees, who transliterates the Hebrew word rather than translating it, seems to have recognized them as a distinct group of people. In 1 Macc. 2.42 they are described as a company (*sunagōgē*), strong in power (*ischuroi dunamei*) (which may mean 'mighty warriors' (NRSV) or more generally 'powerful people', i.e. leading citizens (Kampen, *The Hasidaeans and the Origin of Pharisaism*, 1988, pp. 96-107), who join the friends of Mattathias and organize an army. (They are thus clearly to be distinguished from the group described in 1 Macc. 2.29-38.) In

1 Macc. 7.12 they appear to be identical with or at least associated with
the group (*sunagōgē*) of scribes who trustingly go to the high-priest
Alcimus and the general Bacchides seeking just terms. If they are the
same people as those in 1 Macc. 2.42, they are now, in different circumstances, less ready to fight. The author of 1 Maccabees clearly
thinks them naïve. In 2 Macc. 14.6, however, Alcimus describes the
Hasidaeans as being of much more militaristic mind; under the leadership of Judas they are keeping up war, stirring up sedition, and not let-
ting the kingdom attain tranquillity. This was probably how Alcimus
saw them, and so he killed 60 of them (1 Macc. 7.16). The two authors
approach them with different ends in view: 1 Maccabees is playing
down their importance in favour of the Hasmonaean family, while 2
Maccabees is more concerned to indicate that Judas kept company with
the pious faithful. Their association with the scribes, the interpreters of
the Jewish law, seems assured; their association by some scholars with
the apocalyptic movement and writers is much more speculative. In
what sense they were the spiritual ancestors of the Essenes or the
Pharisees (or in some degree of both) is debatable.

Chapter 2 ends with a speech credited to Mattathias before his death.
Such speeches form a well-established biblical genre (cf. Jacob, Gen.
49; Moses, Deut. 33; Samuel, 1 Sam. 12, and the speeches of Jacob's
sons in the *Testaments of the Twelve Patriarchs*). There are similarities
with the praises of famous men in Ecclesiasticus 44–50, and with the
list of heroes of faith in Hebrews 11. Mattathias describes how, like
Israel's past heroes—Abraham, Joseph, Phinehas, Joshua, Caleb, David,
Elijah, Hanaiah, Azariah and Mishael, and Daniel—Mattathias's family
may be rewarded for their loyalty to the law and covenant. Mattathias
points to victory; vv. 62-63 refers to the coming downfall of the proud
Antiochus. Mattathias finally commends Simeon as the movement's
wise counsellor and father figure, and Judas as the military leader (see
above, p. 25). He blessed his sons, died in year 146 (167–166 BCE), and
was buried in his ancestral tomb at Modein (see further 1 Macc. 13.27-
30). The scene is set; war under Judas may now begin.

Further Reading

On Hellenism and Hellenization
There is a vast range of literature on this topic. The list below includes some of the major
works concerned with the effect of hellenization on the Jews. Recent archaeological
work on this period is producing important results (see articles by Harrison, Peters and
Smith below).

E.J. Bickerman, *The Jews in the Greek Age* (Cambridge, MA: Harvard University Press, 1988).

W.D. Davies and L. Finkelstein (eds.), *The Cambridge History of Judaism*. II. *The Hellenistic Age* (Cambridge: Cambridge University Press, 1989).

L.H. Feldman, 'How Much Hellenism in Jewish Palestine?', *HUCA* 57 (1986), pp. 83-111.

L.L. Grabbe, *Judaism from Cyrus to Hadrian* (London: SCM Press, 1992).

P. Green, *Alexander to Actium: The Hellenistic Age* (London: Thames & Hudson, 1990).

R. Harrison, 'Hellenization in Syria-Palestine: The Case of Judea in the Third Century BCE', *BA* 57.2 (1994), pp. 98-108.

F. Millar, 'The Problem of Hellenistic Syria', in A. Kuhrt and S. Sherwin White (eds.), *Hellenism and the East: The Interaction of Greek and non-Greek Civilizations from Syria to Central Asia after Alexander* (London: Gerald Duckworth, 1987), pp. 110-33.

M. Hengel, *Judaism and Hellenism* (London: SCM Press, 1974).

F.E. Peters, 'Hellenism in the Near East', *BA* 46.1 (1983), pp. 33-39.

R.H. Smith, 'The Southern Levant in the Hellenistic Period', *Levant* 22 (1990), pp. 122-30.

W. Tarn and G.T. Griffith, *Hellenistic Civilisation* (London: Methuen, 3rd edn, 1952)

V. Tcherikover, *Hellenistic Civilization and the Jews* (Philadelphia: Jewish Publication Society of America, 1966; Jerusalem: The Magnes Press, The Hebrew University, 5727).

On 'Antiochenes in Jerusalem'
In addition to discussion in Bickerman (*The God of the Maccabees*), Tcherikover (*Hellenistic Civilization and the Jews*), Hengel (*Judaism and Hellenism*), Goldstein (*I Maccabees*) and other commentaries, see also:

G.M. Cohen, 'The "Antiochenes in Jerusalem", Again', in J.C. Reeves and J. Kampen, *Pursuing the Text: Studies in Honor of Ben Zion Wacholder on the Occasion of his Seventieth Birthday* (JSOTSup, 184; Sheffield: Sheffield Academic Press, 1994), pp. 243-59 .

On the 'Akra':
B. Bar-Kochva, *Judas Maccabaeus: The Jewish Struggle against the Seleucids* (Cambridge: Cambridge University Press, 1989), Appendix D, pp. 445-65.

W. Shotwell, 'The Problem of the Syrian Akra', *BASOR* 176 (1964), pp. 10-19.

Y. Tsafrir, 'The Location of the Seleucid Akra in Jerusalem', *RB* 82 (1975), pp. 501-21.

G. Wightman, 'Temple Fortresses in Jerusalem. Part I: The Ptolemaic and Seleucid Akras', *BAIAS* 9 (1989-90), pp. 29-40.

On Antiochus IV's Decree and the Persecution of the Jews
In addition to Bickerman, Tcherikover and Hengel, and the commentaries, see also:

K. Bringmann, *Hellenistische Reform und Religionsverfolgung in Judäa* (AAWG, Philologische-historische Klasse, 3.132. Göttingen: Vandenhoeck & Ruprecht, 1983).

J. Bunge, 'Die sogennante Religionsverfolgung Antiochus IV Epiphanes und die griechischen Stätte', *JSJ* 10 (1979), pp. 155-65.

L.L. Grabbe, *Judaism from Cyrus to Hadrian* (London: SCM Press, 1992).

E.S. Gruen, 'Hellenism and Persecution: Antiochus IV and the Jews', in P. Green (ed.), *Hellenistic History and Culture* (Berkeley, CA: University of California Press, 1993), pp. 238-74.

F. Millar, 'The Background of the Maccabaean Revolution: Reflections on Martin Hengel's *Judaism and Hellenism*', *JJS* 29 (1978), pp. 1-21.

O. Mørkholm, *Antiochus IV of Syria* (Classica et Medievalia, Dissertationes 58; Copenhagen: Gyldendalske Boghandel, 1966).

P. Schäfer, *Judeophobia: Attitudes towards Jews in the Ancient World* (Cambridge, MA: Harvard University Press, 1997).

On Antiochus IV and his Policies
Those interested in delving behind the biblical portrait of Antiochus IV should read Mørkholm's *Antiochus IV of Syria* (see above), and the following articles by J. Bunge:

J.Bunge, ' "Theos Epiphanes": Zu den ersten fünf Regierungsjahren Antiochus IV Epiphanes', *Historia* 23 (1974), pp. 57-85.

J.Bunge, ' "Antiochus-Helios": Methoden und Ergebnisse des Reichspolitik Antiochus IV Epiphanes von Syrien im Spiegel seiner Münzen', *Historia* 24 (1975), pp. 164-88.

J. Bunge, 'Die Feiern Antiochus IV Epiphanes in Daphne im Herbst 166 v. Chr.', *Chiron* 6 (1976), pp. 53-71.

'The Abomination of Desolation'
In addition to Bickerman, Tcherikover and Hengel, see also:

J. Goldstein, *I Maccabees* (Anchor Bible, 41; Garden City, NY: Doubleday, 1976), pp. 143-57.

H.H. Rowley, 'Menelaus and the Abomination of Desolation', in *Studia Orientalia Ioanni Pedersen septuagenario AD vii id. Nov, anno MCMLIII a collegis, discipulis, amicis dicata* (Hauniae E. Munksgaard, 1953) pp. 303-15.

D. Wenham, 'Abomination of Desolation', *ABD* I, pp. 28-31.

The Hasidaeans
P.R. Davies, 'Hasidim in the Maccabaean period', *JJS* 28 (1977), pp. 127-40.

J. Kampen, *The Hasidaeans and the Origin of Pharisaism: A Study in 1 and 2 Maccabees* (SBL Septuagint and Cognate Studies Series, 24; Atlanta, Scholars Press, 1988).

J. Sievers, *The Hasmonaeans and their Supporters from Mattathias to the Death of John Hyrcanus I* (South Florida Studies in the History of Judaism, 6; Atlanta: Scholars Press, 1990).

5

CHAPTERS 3.1–9.22:
THE ACTS OF JUDAS

The Early Campaigns of Judas

We have already considered the literary structure of this section of 1 Maccabees (pp. 25-26), and here we turn in more detail to the author's presentation of the course of events. The two campaigns described here seem to take place between the death of Mattathias (year 146) and the departure of Antiochus for the Upper Provinces (year 147), and so probably in 167 BCE (see above, Chapter 3). The section is introduced by a poem (3.3-9) celebrating Judas's military prowess, not unlike Ben Sirah's encomium on Joshua (Ecclus 46.1-6), and containing several biblical allusions, including an obvious one to Phinehas in v. 8 ('he turned away wrath from Israel', cf. Num. 25.11). C.F. Burney argues that the opening letters of each verse of the poem, retranslated into Hebrew, form an acrostic on the name 'Jehudah the Maccabee' (*JTS* 21 [1920], pp. 319-25). This presentation of Judas in biblical terms continues throughout the whole section.

The first campaign was begun by Apollonius, unidentified but probably governor of Samaria, as Josephus guesses (*Ant.* 12.287). We are given no details of time or place, but only a brief formal statement of victory and of the death of Apollonius, and the note that Judas took Apollonius's sword and used it in battle for the rest of his life—a clear allusion to David's action after slaying Goliath (1 Sam. 17.51). The second campaign was initiated by Seron, a Syrian army commander, presumably of not too high a rank (cf. v. 14). Judas successfully ambushes him at the pass of Beth-horon, killing 800 troops and putting the rest to flight. There is more detail here (though Bar Kochva [*Judas Maccabaeus*, 1989, p. 215] notes the artificial, laconic character of the narrative), and the basic story is credible, but the author paints the lessons clearly for his readers: Judas's troops are faithful men, Seron's godless (vv. 13, 14); Judas's troops are few, Seron's many, and victory depends not on size but on strength from heaven (vv. 17-19; cf. 1 Sam. 14.6); Seron's troops come in pride and lawlessness, Judas's troops are fighting for their lives and their laws (vv. 20-21). The result is that the Gentiles become afraid of Judas, as the nations feared David after his defeat of the Philistines (1 Chron. 14.17).There is little doubt that 1 Maccabees is presenting Judas as a new David.

The first pair of campaigns (Apollonius and Seron) is separated from the second pair (Gorgias and Lysias, 3.38–4.35) by a report of the reaction of Antiochus IV to the two Seleucid defeats (3.27-37). This report incorporates a certain amount of hard information about Antiochus and his activities (e.g. his need of money, his lavish giving, his appointment of Lysias over the west, with responsibility for Antiochus's son and heir, his division of the army, his departure for Persia in year 147), and some interpretation (e.g. Antiochus's view that his revenue had suffered from his abolition of the Jewish laws, and Antiochus's determination to banish the memory of the people of Israel and Jerusalem from the place by settling aliens there and redistributing the land). The author inevitably presents events from the Jewish viewpoint, even if he has some access to Seleucid sources.

The escalation of war in Judaea continues with the two campaigns of 3.38–4.25 and 4.26-35. 'Lysias chose Ptolemy son of Dorymenes, and Nicanor and Gorgias, able men among the Friends of the king': Ptolemy was in fact the *stratēgos* in charge of Coele-Syria and Phoenicia (cf. 2 Macc. 8.8), and it would have been Ptolemy who appointed Nicanor and Gorgias (cf. 2 Macc. 8.9). We hear nothing more of either Ptolemy or of Nicanor in connection with this campaign, and there is some confusion in the tradition here, for in the 1 Maccabees version the only active general is Gorgias, and in the 2 Maccabees version (8.10-29) the active general is Nicanor. (Gorgias may reappear at 1 Macc. 5.59, and in 2 Macc. 10.14-15; 12.32-37, where he is named as governor of Idumaea.) According to 1 Maccabees, the Seleucid army camps near Emmaus, on the plain, with local slave-traders in attendance hoping for profit. Judas assembles his troops at Mizpah, in the hills north of Jerusalem. Judas's army marches to a position south of Emmaus, while Gorgias moves some of his troops for a surprise attack on the Jewish camp. He finds it empty, and, while he searches the hills for Judas, Judas and his troops attack those left in Gorgias's camp, defeat them, and pursue them to Idumaea, Azotus and Jamnia. When

Gorgias's troops reappear from the hills and see this, they also flee.

1 Maccabees presents a historically credible, but highly coloured picture. 1 Macc. 3.42-60 has the army assembled as a congregation, in the face of its threatened final destruction, ready to fight for people and sanctuary, praying and asking for mercy, fasting, enquiring of the law, bringing out priestly garments, first fruits and tithes, the Nazirites, and making military arrangements after the manner of Deuteronomy (vv. 55-56; cf. Deut. 20.5-9). A lament (v. 45) and a poetic prayer (vv. 50b-53) are introduced, and the preparation ends with a homily from Judas (vv. 58-60). At daybreak, before attack, Judas encourages his men by reminding them of how their ancestors were saved at the Red Sea, and after victory they sang hymns and praises to Heaven, 'for he is good, for his mercy endures for ever' (cf. Ps. 136.23-4). 'Thus Israel had a great deliverance that day' (4.25; cf. Judg. 15.18; 1 Sam. 14.45). This is as fervent a picture as anything in 2 Maccabees, and for all his ability as a historian, the author of 1 Maccabees cannot be accused of impartiality.

The fourth campaign (1 Macc. 4.26-35), led by Lysias 'the next year' with 60,000 infantry and 5,000 cavalry, invaded Idumaea and camped at Bethzur; Judas met them with 10,000 men. The intentional disparity is clear. Judas prays, recalling God's past saving acts by the hands of David and Jonathan (4.30-33), the armies fight, and Lysias's troops are routed. Lysias, observing the Jewish readiness to live or die boldly, returns to Antioch. So little detail is given in this account that many scholars (e.g. O. Mørkholm, *Antiochus IV of Syria*, 1966, pp. 153-54) have suspected it of being a doublet of Lysias's later campaign to Idumaea and Bethzur (6.28-63).

This group of four campaigns, then, shows many signs of the author making the best of limited historical resources. The first and the last have little solid independent content. The first contains little more than the memory of a name, and exists primarily to show Judas in a Davidic glow. The last may be a doublet. The second and third (against Seron and Gorgias) have sufficient topographical detail to be convincing, but the stories have been considerably enriched with religious idealism. None of these war pericopes has any internal evidence of dating; these events are dated only by their positioning between the death of Mattathias (1 Macc. 2.70) and the rededication of the sanctuary (1 Macc. 4.52), and by the dating of Antiochus's campaign to the east (1 Macc. 3.37). These stories are not of themselves enough to convey a full picture of political events between the beginning of the rebellion and the rededication of the sanctuary.

The Cleansing of the Sanctuary

This event is dated by 1 Macc. 4.52 to the 25th day of the 9th month, Chislev, in the 148th year. On the Seleucid Babylonian era calculated from spring 312 BCE, this gives December 165 BCE; on the same era calculated from spring 311 BCE, December 164 BCE. On this latter date, it is unlikely that Antiochus IV could have heard of the event before his death (1 Macc. 6.5-8), and Bringmann argues strongly for the earlier date of 165 BCE. This would mean that the priests restored the sanctuary in autumn 165 BCE, while negotiations were beginning between Antiochus IV and the Jews (see above on the correspondence of 2 Macc. 11, pp. 49-52), which seems quite likely.

According to 1 Macc. 4.42-51 (cf. 2 Macc. 10.2-3), the old, defiled altar was dismantled and its stones carefully stored, and a new altar was built of unhewn stones. The sanctuary and temple interior were rebuilt, the courts consecrated, new vessels made, and lampstand, altar of incense and table of shewbread brought into the temple; incense was burned, the lamps were lit, the shewbread placed on its table (cf. 2 Macc. 1.8), and curtains hung. The dedication of the restored altar was joyfully celebrated for eight days with sacrifices and music (songs, harps, lutes and cymbals) (1 Macc. 4.52-56). 2 Macc. 10.3-8 also mentions the eight days, the sacrifices and the music (hymns of thanksgiving), but adds that the occasion was celebrated 'in the manner of the festival of booths' (cf. 2 Macc. 1.8), and that the celebrants carried ivy-wreathed wands, beautiful branches and palm fronds.

These details have prompted much discussion about the real origin of the festival and the background of its rites. The reference to fire and lights, and the December date, have prompted some to see the feast's origin in the winter solstice, but there is no evidence that any such feast was celebrated in Jerusalem before the Maccabaean era. 'In the manner of the festival of booths' points back to Lev. 23.33-43, and this December feast is clearly modelled on Tabernacles, which began on the 15th day of the month Tishri, October, and had an eight-day celebration, involving sacrifices and the use of the fruit and branches of trees. Also in mind are Solomon's dedication of the altar in the seventh month, as presented in 2 Chron. 7.1-10, and the construction of the altar for the postexilic temple by Jeshua and Zerubbabel in Ezra 3.1-6; on this latter occasion, having set up the altar, they kept the festival of

booths, as prescribed. The particular reference to ivy-leafed wands
recalls the wands (*thursoi*) and ivy leaves (*kissoi*) carried by devotees of
the god Dionysus, and the date of the celebration, the 25th of the
month, was perhaps that of the king's birthday, celebrated monthly.
These two details suggest that the new festival was at least in part a
deliberate counter to these two pagan celebrations (cf. 1 Macc. 1.59;
2 Macc. 6.7).

1 Macc. 4.59 refers to the festival, to be celebrated annually, as 'the
days of the dedication of the altar' (cf. 4.36, 56; 2 Macc. 2.19); the
Greek word used is *enkainismos* (cf. *enkainia* in Jn 10.22) which suggests
rather 'restoration' or 'renewal'. The first-century CE writing *Megillat
Ta'anit* called it *hanukkah*, 'dedication', which may have influenced the
usual translation. 2 Macc. 10.5 speaks rather of 'the purification [Greek,
katharismos] of the sanctuary'. The first letter prefixed to 2 Maccabees
(2 Macc. 1.1-9), dated 124 BCE, instructs Jews in Egypt to 'keep the
festival of booths in the month Chislev'; the second prefixed letter (2
Macc. 1.10–2.18; cf. 2.16) speaks of celebrating the purification of the
temple, but also of celebrating 'the festival of booths and the festival of
the fire given when Nehemiah, who built the temple and the altar,
offered sacrifices' (2 Macc. 2.18). According to this letter, at the time
of exile to Persia priests had hidden some of the temple altar fire in a
cistern; years later, when recommissioning temple and altar, Nehemiah
ordered the priests to find it. They found only a thick liquid, which
burst into flame when sprinkled on the kindling. The author of the letter links this with the festival by noting that Nehemiah and his associates 'called this "nephthah", which means purification' (2 Macc. 1.36).
If this letter, as some think, refers to the first annual celebration of the
new feast and dates from 164 BCE, then the title 'purification' is early,
as is the motif of fire. In any case, these terms are associated with the
festival by c. 100 BCE at the latest. In the first century CE, however,
Josephus knows this feast as 'Lights' (*Ant.* 12.325), explaining the name
'from the fact that the right to worship appeared to us at a time when
we hardly dared hope for it'; he seems almost deliberately to avoid
connecting the name (*phōta*) with the lamps (*phōta*) kindled on the
lampstand (12.319). Abel associates the lamps with the law, arguing that
this meaning became fundamental after 70 CE, when sacrifice ceased.

The Campaigns in Galilee and Gilead (1 Maccabees 5)

1 Maccabees 5 is devoted to campaigns of Judas and others in territories surrounding Judaea: Idumaea, Ammanitis, Galilee, Gilead, Jamnia, the land to the south, and Philistia. It is a distinct block of material, linked to 4.61 by the reference to Idumaea (4.61; cf. 5.3), and to the dedication of the sanctuary by the introduction (5.1-2), but clearly intervening between the rededication (4.36-59) and the death of Antiochus (6.1-17). It is itself an organized collection of stories, with vv. 9-64 at its heart. Verses 9-64 have been coherently planned, as can be seen from the following synopsis:

5.9-15	Pleas for help from Jews in Gilead and Galilee
5.16-20	Arrangements made:
	(i) Simon to go to Galilee
	(ii) Judas to go to Gilead
	(iii) Joseph and Azaraiah to defend Judaea
5.21-23	(i) Simon in Galilee; battles; brings Jews to Judaea
5.24–54	(ii) Judas in Gilead; battles; brings Jews to Judah
5.55-62	(iii) Judas and Azariah are defeated and pursued to borders of Judaea
5.63-64	Judas and brothers honoured in Israel and among Gentiles

Surrounding this central block, the author has placed the following pericopes:

5.3-5	Judas makes war on the descendants of Esau in Idumaea
5.6-7	Judas attacks the Ammonites and takes Jazer
[5.9-64]	[as above]
5.65	Judas makes war on the sons of Esau in the south and struck Hebron
5.66-68	Judas enters Philistia, attacks the cult at Azotus, plunders towns and returns to Judah.

The whole chapter has thus been carefully planned, the central campaigns in Galilee and Gilead (in which Judas gets the lion's share of attention) being flanked by attacks on Idumaea and Transjordan at the beginning and 'the land to the south' and the Philistines at the end. There is no reference anywhere to the date of these events; like the campaigns of chs. 3–4, the date of these events depends entirely on the editorial context. The author of 1 Maccabees may be right in setting these events between the rededication and the death of Antiochus, but the author of 2 Maccabees locates them elsewhere, and in a different

sequence, and neither 1 Maccabees' dating nor sequence should be
taken for granted.

[The relationship of sections of this chapter with similar passages in
2 Maccabees should be briefly noted here. 2 Macc. 8.30-32 seems out
of place between 8.29 and 8.34 (for whatever reason) and is an individual pericope; Goldstein sees these verses as a parenthetical note clarify-
ing Judas's policies after victories (*II Macc.*, p. 320). Bar Kochva (*Judas
Maccabaeus*, pp. 511-12, 514) explains 2 Macc., 8.30-33 as a summary
of Judas's achievements as related in 2 Macc. 12.10-31 (which parallels
1 Macc. 5.24-54). The story in 2 Macc. 10.24-38 may parallel 1 Macc.
5.6-7 (the attack on the Ammonites), 'Gazara' in 2 Macc. 10.32 being
an error for the original Transjordanian Jazer in 1 Macc. 5.8 (Gezer, or
Gazara, west of Jerusalem, probably being an adaptation to the fact that
the event of 2 Macc. 10.24-38 is set in 2 Maccabees in the context of a
campaign against Idumaea). Some scholars have tried to make the
sequence of events in 2 Maccabees the basis for interpreting the order
of events in 1 Maccabees, but the sections in 2 Maccabees relating to
Judas's wars with Timothy, the commander in Transjordan, are as
related so incoherent that it has become necessary to require the existence of two generals called Timotheus in order to make sense of the
narrative. 2 Maccabees has clearly broken up and redistributed its material on Judas and Timotheus. Equally clearly, however, 1 Maccabees
has edited its source material on Judas and Timotheus, and the reconstruction of this campaign, or these campaigns, is probably a lost cause.]

As in his account of Judas's other campaigns, the author of
1 Maccabees makes a point of comparing Judas's military exploits with
similar events in Israel's history. Like King David, Judas attacks the
Edomites (the sons of Esau) and the Ammonites (cf. 2 Sam. 8.13-14;
10.1-14); like King Saul, he rescues Jews from Gilead (cf. 1 Sam. 11.1-
11); like Gideon, he marches his army by night, dividing it into three
companies and frightening the enemy with trumpet-blasts (cf. Judg.
7.15-23); like Moses, he asks for safe passage through enemy territory
(v. 48; cf. Num. 20.14-21) and captures Jazer and its villages (v. 8; cf.
Num. 21.32). The presumption of Joseph and Azariah perhaps reflects
the story of Num. 14.39-45. The Jews are threatened with annihilation
by the Gentiles (5.2, 9), 'in a single day' (v. 27; cf. Est. 3.13), and they
rejoice when they are rescued (5.54; cf. Est. 9.17-19); but as
Deuteronomy had commanded (Deut. 7.2), and as Joshua had done
(Josh. 11.16-20), Judas annihilates his Gentile enemies completely
(5.28, 35, 44, 51). As in 1 Maccabees 3–4, Judas is portrayed in biblical

language as an Israelite hero, fulfilling all that the law required.

1 Maccabees 5 is clearly a carefully tailored literary piece. At its heart lies a number of reports about attacks on places in northern or north-eastern Transjordan—Bozrah, Dathema, Maapha (or Alema, v. 35), Chaspho (cf. Caspin, 2 Macc. 12.13), Maked, Bosor, Raphon, Carnaim, and Ephron, of which only Bozrah and Carnaim can be identified with any certainty. Their location on the map is largely determined by dead-reckoning from their sequence in Judas's supposed route, but how did the author put them in sequence? He seems to know little about these places apart from their names; some are said to be towns, strong and large (v. 26), Dathema is a stronghold (v. 29), Raphon is by a stream (v. 37), Carnaim has sacred precincts (v. 44), Ephron is a large and very strong town commanding the only route, with gates blocked by stones (vv. 46-47). The opening and closing stories, with their reference to the sons of Esau (cf. Gen. 36, with allusion to the Edomites) and the Ammonites and the Philistines, owe as much to Israel's memory of ancient traditional enemies as to any contemporary circumstances; the author's day is represented by reference to Idumaea, Akrabattene (whose position in the region of Samaria rather than Idumaea causes difficulties for the commentator), Beth-shan, Jamnia, Hebron, Marisa and Azotus, all of which are well known. Reconstructing a clear topography and chronology of Judas's campaigns from this chapter is hazardous. The chapter's purpose is to demonstrate Judas's success as a military leader in Idumaea and east of the Jordan, perhaps with an eye to the similar successes of John Hyrcanus (cf. Josephus, *Ant.* 13.254-58).

The Death of Antiochus IV

In 1954 in *Iraq* 16, pp. 202-12, A.J. Sachs and D.J. Wiseman published their translation of a cuneiform tablet from Babylon (BM 35603) originally acquired by the British Museum in the 1880s. This second-century BCE document turned out to contain a list of Seleucid kings from Seleucus I to Antiochus IV. It gives for each the year of accession, the number of years of the reign, and the year of death. Dating is by years of the Seleucid era, calculated from spring 311 BCE. The year in which the king died is counted as the last full year of the reign. The entry for Antiochus IV (and his co-regent, his nephew Antiochus, the son of Seleucus) is as follows (reverse side, lines 10-15):

78 *1 Maccabees*

the same month (= VI, 137 SE) An(tiochus) his son sat on the throne. He
reigned 11 years. The same [year] (= 137 SE), month VIII, An(tiochus) and
An(tiochus) his son ruled as kings. [Year 1]42, month V, at the command of
An(tiochus IV) the king, An(tiochus) the (co-)regent, his son, was put to
death. [Year 14]3, An(tiochus ruled as) king (alone). [Year 148, month] IX, it
was heard that king An(tiochus) [died...]

Seleucus IV died in September 175 BCE, and Antiochus acceded almost
immediately. He put his unfortunate young co-regent to death in
autumn 170 BCE, and news of his own death was reported at Babylon
between 19 November and 19 December 164 BCE. These important
facts give a firm base for the chronology of his reign, and for discussion
of the sequence of events given in 1 and 2 Maccabees. (For this discussion, see above pp. 36-53.) 1 Maccabees dates the dedication of the
new altar before Antiochus IV's death; 2 Maccabees dates the
purification of the sanctuary immediately after it. The view is taken in
this book that 1 Maccabees here as usual is correct.

The account of Antiochus IV's death in 1 Macc. 6.1-16 is a combi-
nation of material from some Seleucid chronicle (6.1-4, 14-16) and
invention by the author of 1 Maccabees (6.5-13). The invention is easy
to recognize. In v. 5-7 the author summarizes chs. 3.38–4.61, and in v.
8-13 he puts into the king's mouth a reflection on the evil he has done
to Jerusalem and Judaea. As vv. 14-16 show clearly, local difficulties in
Judaea were the least of the king's worries. His real concern at that
time was the succession; he wanted power to go to Philip, but in fact it
was Lysias (who had the control of Antiochus IV's son) who took it.
The basic source for the death of Antiochus IV is the Greek politician
and historian Polybius (c. 200–115 BCE) (*Histories* 31.9). Polybius says
that Antiochus, in need of money, mounted an expedition against the
temple of Artemis in the region of Elymais (1 Macc. 6.1 names this as a
city, not a region), but was prevented by the local people. He retreated, fell ill, and died at Tabae between Persia and Media (cf. v. 56). 1
Maccabees tells virtually the same story, and is probably dependent, if
indirectly, on Polybius's version. The letter (2 Macc. 1.10–2.18) containing 2 Macc. 1.13-17 gives a more dramatic version, locating the
incident at the temple of Nanea in Persia, while 2 Macc. 9.1-29 has an
even more dramatic story that Antiochus tried to rob the temples in
Persepolis, was put to flight and retreated to Ecbatana, and died in
anguish far from home on the way to Jerusalem to punish the Jews.
The account in 1 Maccabees is comparatively restrained and accurate.
It does not portray Antiochus as a villain, but has Antiochus show
remorse over his errors in Jerusalem. That Antiochus was 'kind and

beloved' in his rule (6.11) is to some extent borne out by Polybius's account (*Histories* 30.25-26).

Lysias's Second Campaign and Negotiations

The starting point of this episode is the citadel (the Akra; cf. pp. 59-61), which controlled the approaches to the temple, and so was felt as a continuing threat. It is understandable that the Maccabees should wish to remove it, though from the viewpoint of the Seleucids and their supporters it was essential for political control of Jerusalem. Judas's siege of the citadel, and his fortification of the sanctuary and of Bethzur, are reported to the king (now Antiochus V Eupator, now aged about seven and under the control of Lysias), who assembles a large army of infantry, cavalry and elephants, with mercenaries from abroad, and attacks Jerusalem via Idumaea and Bethzur. The date is year 150, which began in spring or autumn 163 BCE (calculating from spring or autumn 312 BCE) or possibly spring 162 BCE (calculating from spring 311 BCE). In fact the attack on the citadel most probably took place in spring 163 BCE and Lysias's campaign in the summer. The year beginning autumn 164 BCE was a sabbatical, or seventh, year (6.49, 53); no crops would have been sown and reaped in spring and summer 163 BCE, and the harvest of 164 would by then have been eaten, so there would be no food left in storage (6.53), and none available in the fields for invading armies to raid—facts that had an important influence on the course of events (6.48-54, 57). Judas tried to block the enemy advance, first at Bethzur (6.31), where the Jews were besieged but in spite of courageous resistance were forced from famine to surrender (6.31, 49-50; vv. 49-50 belong logically immediately after v. 31), and then at Beth-zechariah (Kh. Zakariya, 9 km north of Bethzur), where the Jewish army, caught in an open battle on the plain below Beth-zechariah, was inevitably overwhelmed by the Seleucid war machine. The author makes the best of a bad job, and concentrates on his description of the Seleucid elephants and the bravery of Judas's brother Eleazar Avaran (cf. 2.5), but has to admit that the Jews were afraid and turned in flight (6.41, 47). The Seleucids move up to Jerusalem and besieged the sanctuary, but Lysias called off the siege on hearing that his rival Philip (6.14) had arrived from the east to seize control of the empire. He sensibly made an offer of peace; the Seleucids would allow the Jews to live by their laws, as formerly, if the Jews evacuated the stronghold on Mt Zion (i.e. the fortified sanctuary precincts, cf. 4.60-61). These terms were agreed; but when the Jews left the fortified sanctuary the king, seeing its strength, 'broke the oath he had sworn and gave orders to tear down the wall all round' (6.62). The oath is mentioned in 6.61, but the precise terms are not, and we do not know the Seleucid side of the story.

This section contains much precise detail about Seleucid military matters, and military specialists should consult B. Bar-Kochva, *Judas Maccabaeus*, 1989, pp. 291-346, but the passage as a whole demonstrates well the narrative powers and literary skills of the author. The personal story of Judas's brother Eleazar Avaran (6.43-46) may find an echo in 2 Macc. 13.15. The author's historical sensitivity and relative impartiality is visible in the speeches he credits to the 'ungodly Israelites' from the Akra (6.22-27) and to Lysias (6.57-59). He can see the point of view of loyal Seleucid supporters, and he attributes political sense to Lysias. It is interesting that he makes no mention of Judas in his account of the peace offer; the 'Jews' with whom Lysias deals are unspecified. The letter of 2 Macc. 11.22-26 belongs to this early period of Antiochus V's reign, probably before Lysias's campaign (see p. 50), but possibly at the end of it. The policy expressed in the letter is consistent with that enunciated by Lysias (6.58-59).

Demetrius, Alcimus, Bacchides and Nicanor

From this point, the narrative becomes a more complex tapestry. From 7.1 to 9.22 it describes the political activity in Judaea under the new situation brought about by the arrival of Demetrius as the Seleucid king in Antioch, and the appointment of Alcimus as high-priest in Jerusalem, up to the death of Judas. It is clear that ch. 8, on Judas's dealings with the Romans, has been intruded between 7.50 and 9.1, and we shall consider this under a separate heading below. For the overall structure of this section, see above, pp. 25-26.

If we omit ch. 8, the narrative of 7.1–9.22 may be analysed as follows:

7.1-4	Accession of Demetrius; deaths of Antiochus V and Lysias
7.5-7	Deputation of Alcimus and others to Demetrius
7.8-11	Demetrius sends Bacchides and Alcimus
7.12-18	Alcimus seizes and kills Hasidaeans
7.19-20	Bacchides seizes and kills deserters; leaves Alcimus in charge
7.21-25	Alcimus and Judas; Alcimus returns to king

The first thing to be noted is that, in all this long section, there are only two dates: Demetrius left Rome in the 151st year (1 Macc. 7.1), and Bacchides camped against Jerusalem before the final campaign against Judas in the first month of the 152nd year (1 Macc. 9.3). Since the first date is probably calculated from autumn, and the second from spring 312 BCE, the action takes place between autumn 162 and spring 161 BCE. This may not appear to give much time for these events, but not much time is needed for Bacchides' first visit, and some have suspected that it is a doublet of his second visit. (2 Maccabees ignores it, preferring to concentrate on Nicanor.) There is no indication of how long Nicanor was active in Judaea. The death of Nicanor takes place in the month Adar, i.e. 17 March. The death of Judas was in the first month, presumably April–May of the same Julian year.

The figure of Alcimus is noteworthy. This is 1 Maccabees' first reference to the presence of a high-priest in Jerusalem (Onias, Jason and Menelaus, known to us from 2 Maccabees, have been completely ignored). Alcimus was 'a priest of the line of Aaron' (7.14), and so naïvely trusted by the Hasidaeans; he 'wanted to be high-priest' (7.5), though 'ungodly' he was made high-priest (7.9), and he 'struggled to maintain his high-priesthood' (7.21). He led 'all the renegade and godless men of Israel' to Demetrius (7.5), and broke his oath and committed murder (7.15-16). He did more wrong among the people than the Gentiles had done (7.23), and he laid malicious charges against Judas before the king (7.25). In 9.54, Alcimus is finally accused of tearing down the work of the prophets, and the author notes that he died in great agony (9.56). No other high-priest is mentioned until Jonathan, Judas's brother, is appointed by Alexander Balas (10.20). Only Hasmonaeans, it seems, are satisfactory as high-priests.

The Maccabaean Mission to Rome

Goldstein comments (*I Macc.*, p. 346) that 'If ch. 8 had been omitted, no modern reader would have missed it. Nevertheless, it is an essential part of our author's narrative.' It is linked with the following narrative

by 8.31, and subsequent references to relationships with Rome in
1 Macc. 12.1-4, 16; 14.16, 24; 15.15-24 require the context given by
ch. 8. By the time 1 Maccabees came to be written, Rome was the
pre-eminent power in the eastern Mediterranean, and could not be
ignored; in 63 BCE Roman troops invaded Judaea and entered the temple, and relationships with Rome entered a new and less friendly phase
than that known to the author of 1 Maccabees 8.

Verses 1-16 are in effect pro-Roman propaganda, presumably
directed at Jewish readers under Hyrcanus or his successor. The
author's opening point is that the Romans were 'very strong and well
disposed towards all who made an alliance with them'. Exod. 32.23-33
forbids the Jews to make a covenant (alliance) with foreign peoples
inhabiting the land (cf. Deut. 7.2), but one famous story (Josh. 9.3-27)
sanctioned an alliance with a people who (apparently) came from far
away. The Romans at least qualified on that score (v. 19), as well as on
others. They are good warriors, and control other lands, profitably, by
their planning and patience (vv. 2-4). In particular, the Romans had
defeated Antiochus the Great, father of Antiochus IV, and had dealt
firmly with the Greeks (vv. 6-7, 9-10). While destroying those who
oppose them, they keep friendship with those who rely on them (vv.
11-12). They do not put on crowns or wear purple (the royal trappings
affected by Seleucid kings in particular), but run their affairs by a senate
(like the Jews with their council of elders), and they heed the rule of
one man (as the Jews do their Maccabaean leader) (vv. 14-16).
Throughout the passage, there may be more than a hint of comparison
with the Hasmonaean rulers such as Hyrcanus and Jannaeus, who
themselves began to make conquests in surrounding lands—Idumaea,
the coastal cities, Ituraea and Transjordan.

This essay on the development of the Roman Empire (the details
should be studied in the commentaries) is the author's prelude to his
account of the mission sent by Judas to Rome 'to establish friendship
and alliance' (v. 17). The evidence of 2 Macc. 11.34-38 shows that the
Jews were already known to the Romans, who had considerable interest in the role of the Seleucid Empire in the Mediterranean, and were
perhaps happy enough to profess themselves ready to support the Jews
in certain circumstances, even though the Jews were subjects of the
Seleucid Empire. Rome in fact was not committing herself to much,
and when Demetrius subsequently attacked the Jews they received no
help from Rome. The Jewish mission, however, was successful, and a
copy of the Senate's reply (the original only would have been on

bronze tablets) was sent to Jerusalem 'as a memorial of peace and alliance' (v. 22).

The general authenticity of the reply (vv. 23-30) is agreed, but whether the present text represents a copy of the original decree of the Senate (*senatus consultum*) or of the treaty itself is debated. Verse 22 calls it a 'letter', which might apply to vv. 31-32, which are hardly part of a decree or a treaty. (In any case, this text is presumably the Greek translation of a Hebrew version of the original, which was presumably in Latin.) The phrase 'just as Rome has decided' in vv. 26 and 28 has been taken to reflect the senatorial formula *censuere* ('they voted') and so to indicate an underlying *senatus consultum*, but, if so, the phrase comes oddly in the middle rather than at the end of the separate clauses, and Goldstein speculates that the words indicate a slight departure from the norm in the clause at issue (*I Macc.*, p. 362). Verse 29 has also been suspect as an editorial comment out of place in the text of the treaty. Otherwise the text offers an authentic treaty of friendship and alliance. The first clause establishes peace between the two parties (v. 23). Verses 24-26 and 27-28 require that each side shall bring aid to the other if attacked, and shall not assist the other's enemies—though the requirement that the Romans shall act as allies to the Jews in such circumstances is limited by the let-out phrase 'as the occasion may indicate to them' (v. 27). Additions and deletions can be made by joint agreement (v. 30).

The text of 1 Maccabees 8 itself gives no indication of date, which is usually calculated by reference to a letter from the Roman official Gaius Fannius preserved in Josephus, *Ant.* 14.233. This letter requests safe passage from the magistrates of the island of Cos for some Jewish delegates en route home bearing decrees passed by the Senate. Gaius Fannius [Strabo] may be the consul of that name of 161 BCE (Niese, *Festschrift Nöldeke,* II, p. 817), in which case the mission may be dated 162–161 BCE. The delegates may not have reached Jerusalem before Judas's death (May, 161 BCE).

Further Reading

On the Campaigns of Judas

B. Bar-Kochva, *Judas Maccabaeus: The Jewish Struggle against the Seleucids* (Cambridge: Cambridge University Press, 1989).

J.L. Wallach, 'The Wars of the Maccabees', *Revue internationale d'histoire militaire* 42 (1979), pp. 53-81.

On the Death of Antiochus IV
For problems of chronology, see 'Further Reading' for Chapter 3 above, pp. 52-53. See also

D. Mendels, 'A Note on the Tradition of Antiochus IV's Death', *IEJ* 31 (1981), pp. 53-56.

O. Mørkholm, *Antiochus IV of Syria* (Classica et Medievalia, Dissertationes, 8; Copenhagen: Gyldendalske Boghandel, 1966).

On Hanukkah
F.-M. Abel, 'La fête de la Hanoucca', *RB* 53 (1946), pp. 538-46.

H.E. del Medico, 'Le cadre historique des fêtes des Hanukkah et de Purim', *VT* 15 (1965), pp. 238-70.

J.C. VanderKam, 'Hanukkah: Its Timing and Significance According to 1 and 2 Maccabees', *JSP* 1 (1987), pp. 23-40.

On Roman Policy in the East, and Jewish Diplomatic Dealings with Rome
This subject is discussed by Roman historians rather than by biblical scholars, and much of the literature is to be found in the classical journals.

J. Briscoe, 'Eastern Policy and Senatorial Politics 168–146 B.C.', *Historia* 128 (1969), pp. 49-70.

T. Fischer, 'Zu den Beziehungen zwischen Rom und den Juden im 2 Jahrhundert v.Chr.', *ZAW* 86 (1974), pp. 90-93.

A. Giovanni and H. Muller, 'Die Beziehungen zwischen Rom und den Juden im 2 Jahrhundert v.Chr.', *MH* 28 (1971), pp. 156-71.

E.S. Gruen, 'Rome and the Seleucids in the Aftermath of Pydna', *Chiron* 6 (1976), pp. 73-95.

T. Liebmann-Frankfort, 'Rome et le conflit judéo-syrien (164–161 avant notre ère), *L'Antiquité Classique* 38 (1969), pp. 101-20.

S. Mandell, 'Was Rome's Early Diplomatic Interaction with the Maccabees Legal?', *Classical Bulletin* [Chicago] 104 (1988), pp. 87-89.

B. Niese, 'Eine Urkunde aus der Makkabäerzeit', in C. Bezold (ed.), *Orientalische Studien Theodor Nöldeke zum siebzigsten Geburtstag gewidmet* (Giessen, 1906), II, pp. 817-29.

M. Smith, 'Rome and the Maccabaean Conversions: Notes on 1 Macc. 8', in E. Bammel and C.K. Barrett *et al.*, *Donum Gentilicium: New Testament Studies in Honour of D. Daube* (Oxford: Oxford University Press, 1978), pp. 1-7.

J. Sievers, *The Hasmonaeans and their Supporters from Mattathias to the Death of John Hyrcanus I* (Florida Studies in the History of Judaism, 6; Atlanta: Scholars Press, 1990).

E. Täubler, *Imperium Romanum: Studien zur Entwicklungsgeschichte des römischen Reichs*, I (Leipzig: Teubner, 1913).

D. Timpe, 'Der römische Vertrag mit den Juden im 161 v.Chr.', *Chiron* 4 (1974), pp. 133-52.

W. Wirgin, 'Judah Maccabee's Embassy to Rome and the Jewish-Roman Treaty', *PEQ* 101 (1969), pp. 15-20.

6

CHAPTERS 9.23–16.24:
JONATHAN, SIMON—AND JOHN

Plan and Construction

The third section of 1 Maccabees (1 Macc. 9.23–16.24) continues the story of the Maccabaean struggle for independence through the leadership of Judas's brothers Jonathan and Simon, and ends with a short reference to the part played by Simon's son John immediately after the murder of Simon. These chapters may be summarized briefly as follows (for a fuller synopsis, see above, pp. 27-28).

9.23-34, 43-73	Campaigns of Jonathan against Bacchides
[vv. 35-42	The ambush of the Jambrites]
10.1-89	Jonathan's dealings with Alexander Balas
11.1-19	Defeat of Balas by Ptolemy; deaths of Balas and Ptolemy
11.20-59	Jonathan's dealings with Demetrius II and Trypho
11.60-74; 12.24-38	Jonathan and Simon campaign in Philistia and Galilee, Syria and the coastal plain
[12.1-23	Diplomacy with Rome and Sparta]
12.39-53	Trypho captures Jonathan
13.1-53	Simon's achievements
14.1-3	Persia's capture of Demetrius
14.4-15	Eulogy of Simon
[14.16-24	Diplomacy with Rome and Sparta]
14.25-49	Official honours for Simon
15.1-14, 25-36	Antiochus VII
[vv. 15-24	Roman support for the Jews]
15.37–16.24	Activities of John

This synopsis suggests that the author had a fairly straightforward plan in mind. Jonathan and Simon deal in sequence with Bacchides, Alexander Balas, Ptolemy, Demetrius II and Trypho, and Simon receives a crowning eulogy, balancing the initial eulogy of Judas (3.3-9) (see above, pp. 27-28). But the author at some stage decided to extend his work. He added to the eulogy the official decree in Simon's honour from the Jerusalem archives (14.25-49). He added material about Antiochus VII, in whose reign Simon's son John Hyrcanus, perhaps the author's contemporary and even patron, began his military career. Four further sections appear to have been intruded into this otherwise coherent sequence. The story of the Jambrites (9.35-42) seems to have been built, perhaps at an early stage of composition, into an otherwise clear narrative of an encounter at the Jordan between Bacchides' and Judas's armies (vv. 34 and 43 reveal the editorial linkage). The three sections describing Jewish diplomacy with Rome and Sparta (chs. 12.1-23; 14.16-24; 15.15-24) all sit uncomfortably in the narrative, interrupting the natural sequence of events and causing some problems of chronology; the author seems to have inserted them as well as he could, probably deriving them from a Jewish archive. (Other documents, presumably also from the Jewish archives, such as the letter from Alexander Balas to Jonathan [10.18-20], the letter from Demetrius I to Jonathan [10.25-45], the letter from Demetrius II to Lasthenes, copied to Jonathan [11.30-37], and the letter from Demetrius II to Simon [13.36-40], and the decree giving honours to Simon [14.25-49] seem much better integrated into the narrative and were probably part of it from the beginning.)

There is evidence of some care in the construction of the narrative. In 10.1–11.19, for example, there is a certain artistry in the way in which first Alexander, then Demetrius court Jonathan's support; Alexander kills Demetrius and then courts Ptolemy's support; Ptolemy defeats Alexander, sees his adversary's head, and dies himself three days later. In 11.20-59, the story alternates between Jonathan's relations with Demetrius II (vv. 20-37, 41-53) and Trypho (vv. 38-40, 54-59). In 11.60-74, Jonathan campaigns against Gaza, and Galilee, while Simon takes Bethzur; in 12.24-33, Jonathan campaigns in Syria, while Simon takes Joppa. There is a certain balancing throughout of the deeds of Jonathan and Simon: in 9.62-69 Jonathan and Simon act in concert, as they do against Apollonios (10.74-85). In 11.57-59 Antiochus VI confirms Jonathan as high-priest, and makes Simon governor of the coastal region. In 12.35-38 Jonathan and Simon are associated in building fortifications in Jerusalem and Judaea. In telling of Jonathan's leadership, the author does not let us forget that Simon is at Jonathan's side (cf. also 16.3, in Simon's speech to his sons). In ch. 13, after the capture of Jonathan, Simon becomes leader in Jonathan's

place, tries to ransom him, and builds a tomb for him. Simon's achievements progress via the declaration of independence won from
Demetrius to the capture of Gazara and finally the capture of the Syrian
citadel, the *akra*, and the chapter closes by signalling ahead the future
activities of Simon's son John (13.53; cf. 16.1-10, 18-22, 23-24). The
author has planned the work to underline the contribution of the
Maccabaean family to the development of the later Hasmonaean kingdom. In these chapters, Jonathan and Simon belong together in
achievement (Jonathan is the only other brother named in the decree
honouring Simon, 14.30); Simon's son John is a worthy heir, with
achievements in his own right, but he is briefly portrayed. The focus is
on Jonathan and Simon who were responsible for repulsing Israel's
enemies and establishing its freedom (14.26).

Politics and Documents

It has often been noted that these later chapters are more concerned
with politics than religion. There is comparatively little reference here
to the temple, the law or the practice of religion. It is true that
Jonathan is appointed high-priest (10.20; cf. 11.27, 57) and later Simon
bears the title (13.41), but the author ignores the dubious legality of
this. Demetrius I, in his letter to Jonathan, makes provision for the
repair and upkeep of the sanctuary and for the endowment of its priests
(10.39-44). Jonathan in his letter to the Spartans refers to the high-
priest, the holy books, and sacrifices and prayers offered by the Jews
(12.5-18), and Simon in his speech to the people of Jerusalem reminds
them of his family's activity on behalf of the laws and the sanctuary
(13.3). Simon cleansed Gazara of idolatry and settled observers of the
law there (13.47-48), and the eulogist praises him (14.14-15) for seeking out the law, doing away with the lawless, making the sanctuary
glorious and adding to its sacred vessels. As high-priest, Simon will take
charge of the sanctuary and appoint its officials (14.42). But these
things are not the focus of the story. The author limits himself strictly
to political and diplomatic activity; he notes the topography of campaigns and the terms of agreements and the names of officers and delegates. The author has diplomatic and political rather than ecclesiastical
and religious interests. In this section of the book, there are fewer
prayers (see 11.71; 12.11), and only one poetic piece (14.3-15); on the
other hand, a number of documents are quoted: Alexander's letter to
Jonathan (10.18-20); Demetrius I's offer to the Jews (10.25-45);

Demetrius I's copy to Jonathan of another letter (11.30-37); Jonathan's
letter to Sparta (12.5-18); Sparta's letter to Onias (12.19-23);
Demetrius II's letter to Simon (13.36-40); Sparta's letter to Simon
(14.20-23); the Jewish inscription dedicated to Simon (14.27-47);
Antiochus VII's letter to Simon (15.2-9); the letter of the Roman consul Lucius to Ptolemy and others (15.15-21). The annals of John's
high-priesthood are mentioned in 16.24.

The authenticity of these documents requires examination. As they
stand, they are translations into Greek from the author's Hebrew version of the original Greek or Latin (except for the decree in honour of
Simon, which was presumably in Hebrew or Aramaic, and except for
any document which might have been incorporated when the book
was translated into Greek). We will begin with a scrutiny of the letters
credited to the Seleucid rulers, Balas, Demetrius I, Demetrius II and
Antiochus VII.

Letters from Seleucid Kings

It is probable that Balas's letter to Jonathan (10.18-20) is a précis or
short paraphrase of the original authentic letter; the editor's hand is visible in the intruding parenthesis (v. 20: the intrusion is disguised by the
NRSV translation) noting the sending of robe and crown. The integrity
of the letter of Demetrius I to the Jews (10.25-45) is questioned on
many counts: the awkwardness of order and expression, the similarities
with the letters of Demetrius II in 11.30-37 and 13.36-40, and the
astonishing extent of Demetrius I's concessions to the Jews, including
the handing over of the citadel (which never happened; eventually
Simon captured it). These concessions will be studied further below.
Demetrius II's letter to his right-hand man Lasthenes, with the attached
copy of the letter to Jonathan and the nation of the Jews (11.30-37),
seems authentic, though the precise punctuation and meaning of v. 34
is debated: is the Jerusalem priesthood to receive the benefit of the
income from the three districts transferred to the Jews (NEB and REB),
or is the Jerusalem priesthood being offered tax concessions (NRSV)?
The letter of Demetrius II to Simon (13.36-40) also seems genuine and
appropriate; the release from tribute that it offers (v. 37) means to the
recipients that at long last 'the yoke of the Gentiles was removed from
Israel' (v. 41), and that Israel was independent, as is implied by the
beginning of a new era in v. 42. Antiochus VII's letter to Simon (15.2-
9) is hardly a verbatim copy; it has acquired a 'Hebraic veneer' (Dancy,

A Commentary on 1 Maccabees, 1954, p. 187), visible in the tone of vv. 3 and 9.

However, these Seleucid documents remain important witnesses for the fundamental political concerns of both the Jews and their Seleucid rulers in the final decade of the struggle, and it is interesting to examine their clauses more precisely. The following table (for the letters of Demetrius I, Demetrius II and Antiochus VII) will help.

Clauses	*10.25-45*	*11.30-37*	*13.36-40*	*15.2-9*
Greetings, etc.	25-28	30-31	36	2
Exemption of tribute	29	37		
Exemption of salt-tax and crown levies	29	35b	39	
Exemption of collection of grain and fruit	30	34		
Jerusalem and environs,	31	34		
Tithes and revenues,	31	35		
Holy and free from tax	31			7
Control of citadel given to high-priest	32			
Jewish captives set free without payment	33a			
Taxes on livestock cancelled	33b			
Jews have immunity three days before and after festivals, sabbaths, new moons, etc.	34-35			
Jews can enlist in Seleucid armies, with chances of promotion, and privileges of religion	36-37		40	
3 Samarian districts added to Judaea under high-priest	38	34	(38)	
Ptolemais given to Jerusalem temple for revenue	39			
15,000 silver shekels granted annually by king	40			
Revenues from government for temple resumed	41			
Annual 5000 silver shekels paid from temple revenues to royal officials cancelled	42			
Those seeking asylum in temple for debts to king released and restored	43			
Sanctuary to be rebuilt and restored at royal expense	44			
Walls of Jerusalem and Judaea to be rebuilt similarly	45			
Possession of territory of Judaea confirmed		34		
Gold crowns and palms received (tokens of allegiance)			37	
Validity of previous grants or tax remissions confirmed			38	5
Possession of strongholds built granted			38	7
Cancellation of previous debts	43		39	8
Promise for future of non-cancellation		36		(9)

The chief issue is immediately clear. It is money. Under Antiochus III the Jews had been allowed certain remissions: the Senate, the priests, the temple scribes and singers were exempt from the poll-tax, crown-tax and salt-tax, and the general populace were given tax exemption for three years (*Ant.* 12.142-43). The general payment of tribute, however, must soon have been restored, and under Antiochus IV successive high-priests had (according to 2 Maccabees) offered higher amounts of annual tribute in return for certain benefits. When Demetrius II became king in the 167th year (146 BCE), Jonathan attacked the citadel and asked the king (clearly as the price of lifting the siege) to free Judaea and the three districts of Samaria from tribute (1 Macc. 11.28), in return for which he promised 300 talents (whether annually or as a one-off payment is not clear). The king in response confirmed the possession of Judaea and of the three districts, and apparently offered the temple personnel ('all those who offer sacrifice in Jerusalem') exemption from the royal taxes formerly due to the king annually, from the agricultural taxes (crops and fruits), tithes (the proportional land tax) and other taxes, and salt and crown taxes.

But while the king remits various taxes, he does not appear to remit the annual tribute to be paid by the high-priest on behalf of (and doubtless extracted from) the whole nation. In year 170, Simon wrote to Demetrius asking for relief; Demetrius noted receipt of the gold crown and palm branch, and declared himself ready to offer a general peace and to write to his officials 'to grant release from tribute' (13.37). Any crown-tax owed is cancelled, and 'whatever other tax has been collected in Jerusalem shall be collected no longer'. The Jews celebrate the lifting of the yoke of the Gentiles, which means the lifting not merely of oppression but in particular of the requirement of tribute. Later (1 Macc. 15.5, 8), Antiochus VII confirms all previous tax remissions, and cancels all debts; in 15.30 Antiochus demands payment of tribute money of places that Simon has conquered outside Judaea, but he makes no demand of tribute from Judaea itself.

With this in mind, we can turn back to consider the letter of Demetrius I in 1 Macc. 10.25-45. Demetrius, under pressure from Alexander Balas, makes some of the same concessions repeated later (salt- and crown-tax, agricultural produce collection, tax freedom for the temple personnel of Jerusalem and environs, the cancellation of debts to the king) and adds a large number of other, perhaps lesser, fiscal concessions, such as cancelling taxes on the freeing of slaves, on livestock, on pilgrims travelling to Jerusalem three days before and after a major feast. Astonishingly, he offers control of the citadel to the high-priest (which was hardly expedient), and offers to give the city of Ptolemais to the temple to provide revenue (which was hardly possible), and he offers to rebuild and restore the walls of Jerusalem and of Judaea at royal expense. But above all, he appears to offer the remission of the annual tribute (v. 29)—unless Goldstein (*I Macc.*, pp. 405-406) is right to argue that the *phoroi* (tribute) in v. 29 is not to be construed independently, meaning the annual tribute, but as a noun governing the following salt- and crown-taxes, but this seems to strain the Greek as much as the standard translation. In short, Demetrius's offer seems to go over the top, especially in the light of the subsequent offers of Demetrius II, and it seems probable that Demetrius's original offer has been improved by Jewish wishful thinking.

J. Murphy O'Connor has pointed out that this letter, which is much longer than the others, mixes two different genres of writing. In the body of the letter, vv. 29-30, 32, 33, 34(?), 39-40 are in the first person singular, and vv. 31, 34(?), 35, 36-38, 41-45 are expressed in impersonal style. The former group of verses contains the unlikely offers (including the major tax exemptions, the handing-over of the *akra*, the gift of Ptolemais and the annual grant of 15,000 shekels), while the latter group contains more plausible ones (tax freedom and inviolability for Jerusalem, immunities for pilgrims before and after feasts, permission for Jews to enlist in the army, the transfer of the three Samarian districts, government support for the temple and remission of tax on temple revenues, release for those in asylum on account of debts to the king, and the rebuilding and restoration of the sanctuary, and of the walls of Jerusalem and Judaea). Many of these are substantial offers, but they are appropriate to Demetrius's situation (in view of pressure from Alexander, it would make sense to win Jewish favour by supporting the Jewish temple and its personnel, and also to recruit Jews into the Seleucid army). The suggestion is that these offers form the substance of the original letter. As one might expect, however, they fall short of the total remission of tribute and taxation, and of the granting of independence, which are the promises of Demetrius II, which a Jewish hand has incorporated into the earlier letter of Demetrius I.

This documentary material illustrates both the particular interests of the author of 1 Maccabees and the nature of the struggle between the Maccabees and the Seleucids in the 140s BCE. The Seleucid kings wanted political support and money from their subjects; the subjects

wanted political independence and freedom from the demands of tribute. These documents lie at the heart of the historian's work.

Relations with Rome

A more complicated set of problems arises when we turn to the
author's treatment of the Maccabees' relationships with Rome and
Sparta. It is already clear from the disjointed nature of the narrative (see
above, pp. 27-28) that the author had difficulty ordering and integrat-
ing events (compare, for example, 14.40 with 15.15-24). The fact that
the author treats dealings with Rome and Sparta together, as in 12.1-23
and 14.16-24, adds to the confusion. It may help reconstruction if we
begin by disentangling these activities from each other and from their
context.

In 1 Macc. 12.1, 3-4 Jonathan sends a mission to Rome to confirm
and renew the friendship with Rome originally made in 161 BCE
(1 Macc. 8.17-30). His envoys address the Senate, and they receive letters providing for safe conduct on the return journey. (It is only in a
separate letter to Sparta that we read that the envoys were Numenius
son of Antiochus and Antipater son of Jason, 12.16.) In 14.16-19, we
are told that on hearing of the death of Jonathan and the rule of Simon,
the Romans wrote on bronze tablets renewing the established friendship and alliance. (All commentators note that such an initiative from
Rome is highly unlikely.) In 14.24, 'after this', Simon sent Numenius
to Rome with a gold shield weighing 1000 minas, to confirm the
alliance with the Romans. In 14.38-40, in the decree addressed to
Simon, it is noted that Demetrius II had heard that the Romans had
addressed the Jews as friends, allies and brothers, and had received
Simon's envoys with honour; the author is thus aware that Simon had
sent envoys to Rome, presumably some time at the beginning of his
rule. The return of the envoys (Numenius and his companions) is
described in 15.15; they carry with them a supporting letter from
'Lucius, consul of the Romans' to King Ptolemy and to other rulers,
countries and cities (15.16-24).

The sequence appears confused, and is confusing. We may perhaps
presume (cf. 14.18) that Jonathan's mission was successful and the
friendship renewed. Subsequent events might possibly be restored as
follows: Simon, at the beginning of his rule, sent Numenius and the
shield (14.24), and the Romans responded with their bronze tablets
renewing the friendship and alliance (14.16-19), sending Numenius

back with the supporting letter announcing Rome's support of the Jews to all and sundry (15.15-24). The mission of Numenius (14.24) with the shield would thus precede 14.16, and the return of Numenius (15.15-24), which clearly interrupts the sequence of Antiochus's dealings with Simon and Trypho (15.1-14, 25-36), would precede the decree in honour of Simon, which records that Demetrius II had already heard the news (14.38-40). On this view, the confusion of order could partly be blamed on the intrusion of blocks of material about Rome and Sparta either side of the decree about Simon (14.25-49), and perhaps partly on the fact that the author had no clear information about the dating of the mission to Rome. But the matter is further complicated by the letter which accompanied Numenius, from 'Lucius, consul of the Romans' (15.15-21), which has caused much debate.

This letter is very similar in content to a decree of the Roman Senate preserved by Josephus (*Ant.* 14.145-48) but dated by him to the ninth year of Hyrcanus II (63–40 BCE). The decree was proposed by the praetor, Lucius Valerius, son of Lucius, and ran as follows:

> Whereas Alexander, son of Jason, Numenius, son of Antiochus, and Alexander, son of Dorotheus, envoys of the Jews and worthy men and allies, have discussed the matter of renewing the relation of goodwill and friendship which they formerly maintained with the Romans, and have brought as a token of alliance a golden shield worth fifty thousand gold pieces, and have asked that letters be given them to the autonomous cities and kings in order that their country and ports may be secure and suffer no harm, it has been decreed to form a relation of goodwill and friendship with them and to provide them with all the things which they have requested, and to accept the shield which they have brought.

The link between the two documents is obvious. If 1 Macc. 15.15-24 is part of the original work of 1 Maccabees, it must be dated before c. 100 BCE, and Josephus must have misdated it. If Lucius, consul of the Romans, is the praetor Lucius Valerius of Josephus's document, we have another dating problem, for Lucius Valerius Flaccus was consul in 131 BCE, which would suggest that he held the praetor's office c. 134 BCE, which would be too late for him to be proposing motions in the Senate at the beginning of Simon's rule; 'though unusual, it would not be impossible that he was praetor as early as 143 BCE' (Sievers, *The Hasmonaeans and their Supporters*, 1990, p. 117). We should note also that in Jonathan's letter to the Spartans (12.5-18) the Jewish envoys to Rome are named as Numenius, son of Antiochus, and Antipater, son of Jason (12.16); according to the Spartan letter in 14.20-23, the same envoys were sent to Sparta in Simon's time. To Rome, however, Simon sent Numenius (14.24) or Numenius and companions (15.15), who are not named. They may not have included Antipater son of Jason, and 'companions' suggests more than one person; Josephus's document may therefore rightly name Alexander, son of Jason, with Numenius, son of Antiochus, and Alexander, son of Dorotheus, as the envoys. The problem of the date remains: if Numenius and his companions went to Rome at the beginning of Simon's rule, as seems most likely, then Lucius Valerius's praetorship falls too late for our comfort. If, however, the mission of Numenius and his companions with the gold shield is later in Simon's rule (as 1 Macc. 14.24 and 15.15 might suggest), and is to be distinguished from an earlier mission at the beginning of Simon's rule, then this mission might be dated in the ninth year (as Josephus says)—but the ninth year, not of Hyrcanus, but of the freedom of the Jews, i.e. in 135 or perhaps 134 BCE (Goldstein, *I Macc.*, [1976], p. 479; cf. Sievers, *The Hasmonaeans* [1990], p. 118). This would fit the date of Lucius Valerius's presumed praetorship admirably. We would then, however, have to postulate two diplomatic missions to Rome, one at the beginning of Simon's rule to renew friendship and alliance (mentioned in 1 Macc. 14.16-19, though with no details, and again in the decree, 14.38-40), and another 'after this' (1 Macc. 14.24; 15.15), apparently at the end of Simon's rule, when Numenius and his companions take a gold shield. In this case we may blame the absence of any reference to the return from Rome of the first diplomatic mission (which may be assumed) for the confusion of sequence.

These complications arise from accepting Josephus's association of the decree with Lucius Valerius, son of Lucius, the praetor (Josephus, *Ant.* 14.145). However, if (with Bickermann, *Der Gott der Makkabëer* [1937], p. 175; cf. Timpe 'Der römische Vertrag mit den Juden von 161 v. Chte' [1974], pp. 133-52) we identify the Lucius of 1 Macc. 15.16 with Lucius Caecilius Metellus, one of the consuls at Rome in 142 BCE, all the difficulties disappear, except that of explaining how Josephus connected the letter with Lucius Valerius. In short, no solution seems free from difficulty, and in the end we may have to agree with D. Timpe (1974: 149) that there was one embassy to Rome under Jonathan, another under Simon, but that details of dates and persons remain uncertain.

Contact with Sparta

References to Sparta seem to have been yoked to the material about Rome. In 12.1-4, v. 2 is a clear editorial addition signalling the letter from Jonathan to Sparta in vv. 5-18. This letter refers to an earlier letter sent by King Arius of Sparta to the Jewish high-priest Onias, which is then appended (12.19-23). A similar linkage appears in 14.16-24. In 14.16, an added phrase indicates that Jonathan's death was heard in Sparta as well as Rome. After a note of Rome's reaction, the author gives us a copy of the Spartan letter on the occasion (vv. 20b-23), before returning to Roman affairs (v. 24). For some reason, the author wishes to stress that Jonathan and Simon had good relations with Sparta as well as with Rome. In 146 BCE Rome had defeated the Achaean League and destroyed Corinth, leaving Sparta as the main presence in the Peloponnese, but powerless enough for the future. The suggestion that Jonathan courted Sparta for the sake of her influence with Rome is most unlikely. It is possible that Jonathan wished to show that the Jews had no quarrel with the Hellenistic world as such, now that the battle for independence had been virtually won; but, if so, whom was Jonathan hoping to impress, and why choose Sparta? The Spartans were famous in the ancient world for their militarism, and for their laws, and perhaps for these reasons the Jewish author was anxious to associate the Jewish state, founded on the law and on the military successes of Judas, Jonathan, Simon and John Hyrcanus, with such a famous exemplar. In the late first century CE Josephus saw Moses as the Israelite equivalent of Lycurgus at Sparta *(Apion* 2.154).

The Spartan correspondence must surely belong to the genre of diplomatic fiction. Jonathan's letter (12.5-18) is patently inappropriate and insincere, and the letter he appends, from King Arius to High-Priest Onias (12.19-23), highly improbable. We will take the latter first (because the former depends on it). Arius may be Arius I, 309–265 BCE, in which case Onias is Onias I, high priest c. 300 BCE, or possibly his successor Onias II. Arius I could have known of the ancestral Spartan link with Egypt through Danaus from the fifth-century BCE historian Herodotus (*Histories* 6.53; 2.91); he could also have known from Hecataeus of Abdera (c. 300 BCE) that at a time of pestilence the Egyptians had once ejected aliens, including both Danaus and the Jews, from Egypt. Whether Arius could have deduced from this the kinship of the Spartans and Jews, and where he might have found reference to Abraham, are uncertain. (There is no reference to Abraham in the extant remains of Hecataeus.) However, there seems little reason why Arius I, c. 300 BCE, should have wished to contact the obscure region of Judah under Ptolemaic control; if the letter were authentic, Josephus's identification (*Ant.* 12.225) of the addressee as the high-priest Onias III (murdered c. 172 BCE) would be more plausible, but there was no contemporary Spartan king called Arius. The proposal of reciprocal property rights (v. 23) is reminiscent of 1 Kgs 22.4; 2 Kgs 3.7, and most unlikely between Sparta and Judaea.

This letter, in spite of some scholarly attempts to authenticate it, is a diplomatic invention, used in support of Jonathan's letter of 12.5-18. This letter also is highly suspect, not only because it is patently insincere (vv. 11-12), but because in vv. 13-14 the author, writing shortly after a major upheaval in Greece, focuses only on Jewish sufferings and reveals a totally undiplomatic lack of concern for Sparta's troubles. The reference to the sending of Numenius and Antipater to Rome, 'and also to you' (vv. 16-17), betrays a similar lack of diplomacy, and arouses again the suspicion that the author is basing his Spartan material on the far more authentic record of diplomacy with Rome. The final letter in this series, the Spartan response in 14.20-23, is again set into the account of Simon's diplomacy with Rome. The reference to the visit of Numenius and Antipater creates serious difficulties for the chronology (see Dancy, *A Commentary on 1 Maccabees*, 1954, 182-83), and depends on the earlier reference in 12.16. These two letters were almost certainly composed by the author of 1 Maccabees and linked to the material about Rome, and they have added to the confusion of the narrative.

These findings, however, do not rule out the possibility of diplomatic contact between Sparta and Judaea; we know that nearly three decades earlier the high-priest Jason had fled to Sparta (2 Macc. 5.9), and according to 1 Macc. 15.23 the Romans sent a letter of support for the Jews to the Spartans in Simon's time. The author of 2 Macc. 5.9 comments that Jason fled 'in hope of finding protection because of their kinship' (2 Macc. 5.9), and clearly knows the alleged relationship. This brings us back to the letter attributed to Arius, quoted also in slightly extended form—and so perhaps not from 1 Maccabees—by Josephus (*Ant.* 12.225-27), and it seems most likely that this letter, though inauthentic in the sense that it was attributed to rather than written by Arius I, was available for use by the author of 1 Maccabees. It was not unusual for cities of the Hellenistic world to claim interrelationships on legendary or historical grounds (cf. Dancy, *1 Maccabees*,

1954, p. 166). Josephus may be right to relate the letter to the period of Onias III; the letter could even have been useful to Jason. The name Arius was given as the best-known Spartan king of Hellenistic times. This suggests (as does the reference to Abraham) that the letter was invented from the Jewish side. It is one more piece of evidence for the increasing Jewish interest in association with the wider Hellenistic world in the early decades of the second century BCE.

The Decree in Honour of Simon

Lastly, we should consider the decree addressed to Simon (1 Macc. 14.27-45). Like other documents, this was apparently recorded on bronze tablets (cf. 8.22; 14.18), which were mounted on pillars on Mt Zion (14.27). The author claims to give the text of what was written (Greek, *tēs graphēs*, v. 27; *tēn graphēn tautēn*, v. 48) in vv. 27-45. Honorific decrees are well known from the Hellenistic world. They usually take the obvious form of recording, first, the honorand's achievements in a series of clauses beginning 'whereas…' (Greek, *epeidē*), and secondly, the decree of the body awarding the honour, introduced by 'it seemed good to…' (*edoxe…*). In the present document, after a preamble giving the date and place of the proclamation, Simon's achievements are listed in vv. 29-40, beginning with a clause introduced by 'since' (Greek, *epei*). These verses in fact form a continuous narrative of Simon's achievements rather than a series of 'whereases', and they include a report that the people had already made Simon their leader and high-priest (v. 35), and a further report that Demetrius had confirmed Simon in the high-priesthood (v. 38), before we reach the second part of the document (v. 41) which narrates that the Jews and their priests have resolved that Simon should be their leader and high-priest forever, that he should be governor, with various powers (vv. 41-43). The final verses seem to give the direct speech of the decree as it affected the people and the priests (vv. 44-46). Verses 46-49 report the people's acceptance of Simon's rights, Simon's acceptance of his official responsibilities, and the orders to inscribe and display the decree.

This passage thus displays a mixture of direct and indirect speech; the author of 1 Maccabees appears at points to be quoting, at points to be reporting the decree. Verses 27b-28 and 29-34 appear to be direct quotation (though if the decree was originally couched in the third person, 'proclaimed to us' in v. 28 reads strangely). Verses 35-37, 38-

40 might be direct quotation, but vv. 35-36 (as far as 'toward his nation') and vv. 38-40 read more as a report of the actions of the people and King Demetrius, which are perhaps surprising in an official Jewish decree of 'the Jews and their priests'. The presence of vv. 38-40 at this point, as we have seen, may cause complications for the chronology of Simon's diplomatic activities. Verse 41 is particularly strange, because the Greek text introduces the clause in such a way as to make it a continuation of what Demetrius had heard. This cannot be right; if the author of 1 Maccabees is quoting the original decree, what is required here is direct (not indirect) quotation of the decree in the present (not past) tense: 'In view of all these things, it seems good to the Jews and their priests...', i.e. 'be it resolved that...' (Goldstein, *I Macc.*, 1976, p. 507).

There is evidence, then, that the author has adjusted the original text, perhaps mainly to serve the needs of his narrative. But what is more important is what is said and what is not said, and what the decree reveals of the political situation. It is sometimes said that the decree says nothing of the events of chs. 1–9, but is this true? Verses 29 and 32 tell of the energy of Simon, son of Mattathias, and his brothers on behalf of the law and the sanctuary, when enemies decided to invade and lay hands on the sanctuary. This surely refers to the earlier events; no enemy attacks the sanctuary after Judas has restored it. There is no direct reference to Judas, and the reference to Jonathan in v. 30, between vv. 29 and 31, seems out of place, and may be intruded into the decree by the author of 1 Maccabees, who seems anxious to see Jonathan and Simon as a pair acting together. The original decree emphasized to the exclusion of all others the role of Simon, as natural in a decree dedicated to his honour.

The author of 1 Maccabees is also concerned to show that the people (v. 35) had a hand in Simon's elevation to leadership and high-priesthood (cf. 13.41-42, which suggests that this happened in his first year and not in his third, as the decree suggests), and he is concerned to note also that Demetrius II confirmed Simon in this office (v. 38). He wishes further to include the fact that Simon was honoured by the Romans (v. 40). These points were probably not foremost in the mind of 'the Jews and their priests' who proposed the decree (v. 41). The phrase 'the Jews and their priests' is an unusual one, particularly at this point in a formal assembly consisting of the priests, the people, the rulers of the nation and the elders of the country (v. 28), and one wonders who exactly is meant (cf. Sievers, *The Hasmonaeans and their*

Supporters, 1990, p. 123). Perhaps we should think particularly of the priests, whose support would have to be for the high-priest. Those proposing the decree, however, were not concerned with the role of the people or of Demetrius II, but surely sought by honouring Simon to strengthen their own position, and to underline their own role in the constitution. And though Simon is given enormous powers as leader (*hegoumenos*), high-priest (*archiereus*), governor (*strat gos*), with care of the sanctuary, with administrative control of the country, its armaments and fortifications, commanding the obedience of all, the authority behind all contracts, with the sole right to wear purple and gold, nevertheless there are controls. His political and priestly office are subject to the possibility that a prophet might arise to condemn his rule or appoint another ruler, or bring in the kingdom of God; and his appointment 'forever' probably refers not to the establishment of a dynasty but to a personal life appointment. For all the purple and gold, and though opposition and the convening of assemblies without his permission are forbidden, Simon is not declared king; he has not that ultimate power. That power was taken by a later generation of Hasmonaeans.

Dynastic Continuance

The author of 1 Maccabees emphasizes (14.49) that the terms of the decree were to be available to Simon and his sons. There are earlier references to Simon's sons: in 14.53, Simon notes that his son John has reached manhood, makes him commander of the army, and settles him in Gazara. In 14.25 the people ask, 'How shall we thank Simon and his sons?' In the final chapter of his book the aged Simon calls his eldest sons Judas and John and invites them to 'Take my place and my brother's, and go out and fight for our nation, and may the help that comes from heaven be with you' (16.3). John's skill in battle and his decisive action at the crisis of the assassination of his father are demonstrated, and the book ends with the brief notice that

> The rest of the acts of John and his wars and the brave deeds that he did, and the building of the walls that he completed, and his achievements, are written in the annals of his high priesthood, from the time that he became high priest after his father (16.23-24).

The author knows more than he tells. He has no wish to write the history of John Hyrcanus, but he does wish to indicate that John was a chip off the old block, and that the Hasmonaean process is continuing.

Further Reading

On Letters from the Seleucid Rulers:
In addition to the commentaries of Abel, Dancy, Goldstein, etc.:
J. Murphy O'Connor, 'Demetrius I and the Teacher of Righteousness (1 Macc.x.25-
    45)', *RB* 83 (1976), pp. 400-20.

On Relationships with Rome and Sparta
B. Cardauns, 'Juden und Spartaner: Zur hellenistisch-jüdischen Literatur', *Hermes* 95
    (1967), pp. 317-24.
T. Fischer, 'Zu den Beziehungen zwischen Rom und den Juden im 2 Jahrhundert
    v.Chr.', *ZAW* 86 (1974), pp. 90-93.
M.S. Ginsburg, 'Sparta and Judaea', *CP* 29 (1934), pp. 117-22.
A. Giovanni and H. Muller, 'Die Beziehungen zwischen Rom und die Juden im 2
    Jahrhundert v.Chr.', *MH* 28 (1971), pp. 156-71.
R. Katzoff, 'Jonathan and Late Sparta', *AJP* 106 (1985), pp. 485-89.
S. Schüller, 'Some Problems Connected with the Supposed Common Ancestry of Jews
    and Spartans and their Relations during the Last Three Centuries BC', *JSS* 1 (1956),
    pp. 257-68.
D. Timpe, 'Der römische Vertrag mit den Juden von 161 v.Chr.', *Chiron* 4 (1974), pp.
    133-52.

On the Decree for Simon
In addition to the commentaries of Abel, Dancy, Goldstein, see:
J. Sievers, *The Hasmonaeans and their Supporters from Mattathias to the Death of John Hyrcanus*
    (Florida Studies in the History of Judaism, 6; Atlanta: Scholars Press, 1990).

7

EPILOGUE:
THE HISTORIAN

From this study the author of 1 Maccabees emerges with credit as a serious historian. The material of 1 Maccabees is well organized and structured, its chronology is based on official dates, its sequence is for the most part coherent and reliable. The author has made good use of the sources available, in the section devoted to Judas relying partly on what were probably oral accounts of Judas's exploits, and in the section devoted to Jonathan, Simon and John, making much use of archival material and official records. It is true that, as we have seen, these letters and documents show signs of editorial adjustment. However, the Seleucid correspondence is basically authentic, though Demetrius I's letter to Jonathan has been heavily reworked and Antiochus VII's letter to Simon has acquired a 'Hebraic veneer'. The Roman treaty of ch. 8 and the contents of the letter of Lucius are authentic enough, though there remain problems with the dating and sequence of the missions to Rome. The Spartan correspondence is another matter. Here the author of 1 Maccabees has used a pre-existing but fictional letter as the basis for reconstructing appropriate correspondence and has clumsily integrated it into the account of diplomatic dealings with Rome. The decree honouring Simon has been slightly edited to link up with historical details already given in the text.

Thus apart from Demetrius I's letter, into which the historian has brought forward fundamental negotiating points from the later letters of Demetrius II, presumably believing that these concerns were urgent from the start of negotiations, and the Spartan correspondence, which is partly invented for the occasion, the author has done nothing more than edit the available documentary sources into the text. On the other hand, it must be admitted that the author often has to incorporate accounts of campaigns and other events for which he has no certain or precise date into his story—for example, the early campaigns of Judas in chs. 3–4, the campaigns against neighbouring peoples in ch. 5, the mission to Rome in ch. 8, and the campaigns of Jonathan in Galilee and Syria in chs. 11 and 12. Many individual stories about Judas and Jonathan, probably deriving from oral tradition, had no precise date attached to them, and the author had to work out how best to fit things together within a framework mainly supplied by official Seleucid dates. The author was a responsible historian, properly concerned to present the story in as orderly a way as possible, and can be credited with considerable historical objectivity and width of vision. For example, he offers a comparatively balanced picture of the political concerns of the Seleucids and Romans. The author recognizes the value of the Romans and the Spartans to the Jews, and has some knowledge (though the list of 15.23 perhaps suggests a limited geographical sense) of the cities and politics of the wider Hellenistic world. 1 Maccabees is the work of a convinced nationalist, who sees the history of the Maccabaean age as a continuation of the earlier history of Israel as seen in the books of Kings and Chronicles, but who is equally aware of both the difficulties and advantages of Jewish relationships abroad.

This book has studied the work of 1 Maccabees and has carefully avoided reading 1 Maccabees in the light of 2 Maccabees. If we want to write the history of the Maccabaean family and era, we must begin by seeing it through the eyes of individual historians who have left us their separate interpretations of it. It is unlikely that the historian of 1 Maccabees knew the work of the Epitomist or of his source, Jason of Cyrene, and it is important to try to understand the picture given by 1 Maccabees without confusion from 2 Maccabees. The present study makes clear that the modern historian must treat the ancient historian of 1 Maccabees with great respect.

Indexes

Index of References

Bible

Old Testament

Genesis
36	77
49	67

Exodus
20.4-6	62
23.24	65
28.1-39	31
32.23-33	82

Leviticus
23.33-43	31, 73

Numbers
20.14-21	76
25	66
25.11	70
28.3-8	62

Deuteronomy
5.8-10	62
7.2	76, 82
7.25-26	65
12	62
18.14	32
20.5-9	72
20.5-8	31
33	67

Joshua
9.3-27	82
11.16-20	76

Judges
7.15-23	76
15.18	72

1 Samuel
11.1-11	76
12	67
14.6	71
14.45	72
17.51	70

2 Samuel
2.19	31
4.4	64
7.15-16	31
8.13-14	76
10.1-14	76

1 Kings
22.4	96

2 Kings
3.7	96
19.35	31
21.2-5	65

1 Chronicles
14.17	71
24.7-18	31

2 Chronicles
7.1-10	73

Ezra
3.1-6	73
6.8	31
7.10	31
7.20	31

Nehemiah
7.65	32

Esther
3.13	76
9.17-19	76

Psalms
37.10	32
37.35-36	32
44	32
74	32
79	32
79.2	66
79.3	32
118	32
136	32
136.23-24	72
149.1	66

Isaiah
11.1	55
14.12-14	55

Ezekiel
2.6	18
28.2-10	55
34.27	32

APOCRYPHA

11.34-38	47, 51,	12.24-38	76	14.1	49
	82	12.32-37	71	14.4	49
11.34	51	12.43-45	31, 45	14.6	66, 67
11.35	51	13.1-3	47	14.37-46	48
12.2-38	48	13.1	49	15.1-36	48
12.10-31	76	13.9-26	47	15.6-36	47
12.13	77	13.15	80	15.37-39	45, 48

OTHER ANCIENT REFERENCES

Pseudepigrapha		13.227	17	5.136-41	60
1 Enoch		13.254-58	77	5.137	60
85–90	34	14.145-48	93	5.138	61
		14.145	94	5.139	61
Josephus		14.233	83	5.252	60, 61
Ant.		20.12.1	17	5.354	60, 61
12.138-46	55			13.215-17	61
12.142-43	90	*Apion*			
12.225-27	96	1.7-8	16	Christian Authors	
12.225	96	1.9	17	Eusebius	
12.235	74	1.37-44	16	*Hist. Eccles.*	
12.242–13.212	16	2.154	95	6.25	17
12.252	60, 61				
12.260-61	62	*Life*		Classical Authors	
12.265	18	65	17	Herodotus	
12.287	70			*Histories*	
12.319	74	*War*		2.91	95
12.362	61	1.3	18	6.53	95
13.214	17	1.39	60	30.25-26	79
13.223-25	17	1.50	61	31.9	78
				31.56	78

INDEX OF AUTHORS